Mini Farming for Beginners:

The Ultimate Guide to Remaking Your Backyard into a Mini Farm and Creating a Self-Sustaining Organic Garden

Contents

Introduction

Gardening is an extremely fulfilling activity that allows you to reap the fruits of your own labor. If you have a backyard and want to turn it into a mini farm but don't know where to begin, this is the right book for you. What makes this guide different from other books is that it will help you every step of the way, until you can harvest produce from your garden. This book is equally helpful for beginners and those who have experience with gardening or farming. You will learn everything from how to prepare the soil, choose the right plants, and set everything up to protect your plants from any pests or diseases. The best part is that you will be able to do it all organically.

Organic produce is not only good for your body, but it also allows you to maintain the integrity of the soil and underground water. You can utilize the space you already have to grow your garden effectively and feasibly. It does not require much investment; rather, it will help you to save a lot of money in the long run. You will see your grocery bills go down and save on food expenses. You can even sell your excess produce at the farmers' market if you want to.

Organic produce allows you to protect the environment, since you reduce chemical usage. The produce obtained will also be free of any hidden additives or chemicals and pesticides that seep in when grown commercially. Foods with such hidden ingredients can harm your health in the long run. Instead, when you rely on organic materials, not only do you get healthier plants, pests and diseases are less likely to attack and destroy your crops.

Being able to grow healthy organic food in your own backyard can be a blessing. It is not as expensive as you may think, nor is it complicated. As you learn more about organic gardening, you will want to get started as soon as possible. So, without much ado, start reading and take the first steps toward a bountiful mini farm in your own backyard.

Chapter One: If You Have a Yard, You Can Farm

The first step to get started is to evaluate the backyard space you have available for the farm, as it will determine the various styles of farming you can use. You can choose from no-till "lasagna gardening"; raised beds; aquaponics; and hydroponics. Even with small spaces, there are many options available, such as container gardening and vertical gardening. Although livestock and beehives can be added, the best advice for beginners is to start small and gradually expand and include them.

Anyone can start a farm in their backyard regardless of its size. As long as you utilize the space well, you can grow a number of different fruits, vegetables, and herbs, which will sustain you throughout the year. You can even raise livestock if you want, but it is best for beginners to start small.

Once you have evaluated what space you have, decide which type of farming will be best. While you can go down the commercial route too with your small farm, the important thing to consider is sustainability. This will allow you to farm, raise, and grow everything you need in your backyard. Having five acres of land is ideal, but even a single acre can allow you to be completely self-reliant. Regardless of how much space you have, you can start a mini farm.

Benefits of Backyard Farming

Backyard farming has many benefits; some of them are mentioned below.

It Is Easy to Manage

It is easy to manage the plants that you grow in your backyard. You can conveniently go and check on or harvest the products whenever you want. You don't need to call any professionals or farmers to check on your farm, since you can do it yourself. You have access to your own garden and can see if your plants are growing well or not.

It Is Better for Your Health

Your health improves when you consume more freshly grown fruits and vegetables. You can pluck them directly from your backyard whenever you want. It also allows you to maintain the quality of your products by ensuring that everything is done organically without using any pesticides or chemicals.

It Will Help You Save Money

When you grow your own produce or raise your own livestock, you don't have to spend money at grocery stores. Your grocery bills will reduce significantly. Organic vegetables, in particular, can be expensive to purchase, but growing them will cost next to nothing.

You Will Get More Exercise

Farming is an activity that keeps you active and gives you productive results. All the digging, planting, maintenance, etc. will help you burn a lot of calories. It is also good for your mental health and will keep you in a positive state of mind. Gardening is a stress-relieving exercise and also provides physical exercise.

You Will Contribute to Better Environmental Conditions

Urban farming helps to cut down on the fossil fuel consumption usually caused by the transportation, packaging, and selling of food.

You can reduce your carbon footprint by being self-dependent for your food growth.

How to Grow More in Small Spaces

You may think that your yard is not big enough, but this is not true; if you have a yard, you can farm. Various techniques allow you to utilize the smallest of yards in the best ways possible. With some ingenuity and creativity, you can maximize the smallest spaces for greater yields. People in urban areas have started growing food successfully on their balconies as well, so if you have a backyard, there are a lot more possibilities to explore.

Here are some ways in which you can grow more in your mini farm:

Container Gardens

A container garden is a great option for someone who has limited outdoor space. The great thing about container gardens is that you can grow nearly any vegetable and many different types of fruit in them. As long as the conditions are optimal and the container is appropriately sized, you can grow plants.

If you provide the plants with adequate sunlight and proper watering, it is possible to grow some small fruit trees in containers as well. Some people grow blueberry bushes and lemon trees successfully in this way. Container gardening will ensure that you use every inch of space because all the soil in the containers is used for the production of vegetables or fruits. Growing space is not wasted in any way if you just care well for the plants.

It also saves you from the stress that is usually placed on your back from bending over ground plants. People who have back problems should consider using container gardening techniques. It is less physically straining and an accessible gardening technique for everyone.

Another benefit is that the containers can be moved around, which allows you to ensure that the plant is always getting proper light.

Certain plants thrive well even under shade or with dappled sunlight, but others need at least six hours of direct sunlight. You can chase the sun with your containers if required.

You don't always have to buy containers for container gardening. Consider up-cycling and using things you already have. You can even use plastic totes as planters if you are not too concerned about aesthetics. Kitchen herbs grow well in steel pasta strainers. There are many such ways in which you can create your own gardening containers.

The important thing to remember is that any container should allow proper drainage. So, if you use a tin can or an old bucket, drill some holes in the bottom to allow excess water to flow out. If the container has enough space, almost any plant can be grown in it. You can use straw bales too, but these break down quickly and are messy. However, these are a viable option, and plants such as zucchini or pumpkin can be grown in them.

When you use containers, it is important to add fertilizer and water them more often since the soil will dry out faster in them. The nutrients get flushed out at greater speed, too, when compared to soil on the ground. Nonetheless, container gardening is a popular way to grow plants in smaller spaces.

Vertical Gardening

Plants can be grown upwards in so many different ways. In fact, most fruit or vegetable bearing plants grow in an upward direction. If you have a small yard, try options such as a hanging hydroponic garden, recycled pallet planter, or a traditional trellis. You just need a little creativity since there are a lot of options. Using space productively is key in a small yard.

Here is a list of the plants that grow well in vertical planting:

Tomatoes

Cherry tomatoes will grow particularly well if you grow them upwards with adequate support. Other varieties of tomatoes also grow well if the right support is provided. You can cut old nylons and use this fabric for tying the plant to the upward structure. These are flexible and will not induce much stress on the points where the plants are attached. You can make these strips yourself or buy some material from a thrift store at a very small price. You can also plant along a wall and watch as the tomatoes grow all through the summer.

Melons and Winter Squash

These are natural vines and grow well when planted upwards. Just add some good support and train the plant to grow upward. It is particularly important to ensure that the support structure is strong when the plant is about to bear fruit.

Pole Beans and Peas

If you add some proper support, these grow upwards quite easily.

Cucumbers

These plants are easy to grow and don't need much space either.

Square Foot Gardening and Raised Beds

If you have enough space for raised beds, you can make better use of your yard. Raised beds allow more plants to be grown in every square foot of space. They are also a great way to reduce the growth of weeds. Weeding is much easier from a raised bed as you don't have to bend very low, and your back is not strained. Even people with reduced mobility can easily care for a raised bed garden if there is adequate spacing to allow movement. Raised bed gardening makes the upkeep of the garden much easier for everyone. Raised beds are ideally about twenty inches deep. However, if you are building the raised bed over the soil, there is some leeway.

Raised bed gardening has many benefits:

• The growing season is extended. The ground takes longer to warm up in spring and fall, as compared to a raised bed, which warms up faster. You can tend the bed so that the growing season is extended a couple of weeks.

• Regardless of what the natural soil conditions are in some parts of your yard, you can still grow food thanks to a raised bed. You can add high-quality soil to the bed and utilize the space well.

• The drainage factor in raised beds is great. Regardless of where the garden is, there will be good drainage.

• The problem of soil compaction is solved. You can easily work and maintain the soil even in a small space.

• Every inch of space will give you food. You won't be wasting any space underfoot if you grow plants in a raised bed.

• You can build the height of the bed according to your needs, to reduce back pain.

Keyhole Gardening

Keyhole gardens are another way to make maximum use of space, since they eliminate the need for walkways. In traditional gardening or even with raised beds, you have to keep enough space for movement around the garden. Keyhole gardens are resistant to drought and you can nurture the plants with compost throughout the whole season. A keyhole garden is a raised bed that is in the form of a circle and has a path shaped like a keyhole that allows access to the whole garden. There is a vertical tunnel in the middle of the circle that will have many layers of compost. The compost keeps breaking down and thus directly provides nutrients and moisture to the bed. Many different materials can be used for building such keyhole gardens.

Edible Perma-Scaping

In this method, you can plant perennial plants that bear food instead of ornamentals that are usually grown in those spaces. Most popular ornamental plants are actually edible, so it is not difficult to turn your landscape into one that also provides food. You should consider your whole yard as a possible space to grow produce, since this will increase your yield.

Lasagna Gardening

This is a simple way of turning your backyard into an organic garden that will provide food for you. Lasagna gardening has nothing to do with pasta or its ingredients. It is a technique that is also called "sheet composting" or "sheet mulching." It helps to prevent food wastage and allows you to grow produce in your yard quite quickly. You don't have to buy soil for this method either. Even if your yard has heavy clay soil, you can use this method to grow organic vegetables or fruit easily. Soil, root barriers, and mulch are layered over the grass in the yard. The layering is done in such a way that the plants can obtain nutrients from the soil below and moisture is retained but weeds are not able to grow through easily.

Hydroponics

In hydroponics, you will use a nutrient solution instead of soil to grow your plants. This is a good way to grow plants where your soil is of low quality, or you don't have enough space. The roots of the plants will obtain nutrients from the solution instead of being under the soil. Certain mediums such as "coconut coir" or coconut fiber and gravel are also used in this method. There are many hydroponic systems that you can choose to apply to your farm. You can build a continuous flow system where nutrient solution is constantly flowing through the roots, and this allows the plants to absorb oxygen better. You can also have a static solution in containers such as buckets where the plants are grown without the water being aerated. In an aeroponic system, the plants will only be misted using the nutrient solution and not immersed in the solution. Hydroponics will allow you to diversify your mini farm and can be used to grow many different plants in a greenhouse or indoors throughout the year.

Aquaponics

Aquaponics in a farm combines hydroponics and aquaponics. Aquaponics has been used since ancient times when Chinese farmers grew paddy fields and fish such as eels and carp together. Bacteria convert the fish produced waste into nitrates that feed the plant. Your aquaponic system will usually consist of a tank where the fish are reared; a hydroponic system; a settling basin for capturing the unused fish food; a biofilter with bacteria; and a pump that pumps water through the system.

Many other methods are adopted by small farmers around the world to optimize their space and get the maximum yield from their farms.

Starting Your Backyard Farm

You can start transforming your yard into a hyper-productive farm instead of letting the space waste away. It will allow you to maximize your resources, save money, and increase the yield from your garden. If you want to be more self-sufficient, having a mini farm in your backyard is the solution. It does not matter if you have a tiny lot or acres of land. The key is to plan and execute it efficiently.

Reduce the Lawn Area

Your lawn will usually require watering, feeding, weeding, and regular mowing. Most communities have rules regarding outdoor watering. You also have to consider the environmental implications of emissions from mowers that are gas-powered, chemical fertilizers, et cetera.

If you reduce a lot of your lawn area, it helps you to turn your yard into a more earth-friendly space. You can tear out the turf and replace it with water-wise grass or ground covers that are drought resistant. It will allow you to reduce water wastage and still enjoy the yard. But what you should do is go one step further and turn the space into a vegetable garden. Since the lawn was already cared for, the soil will be great to grow abundant produce. It requires effort and time to grow a food garden, but it is worth the investment. You will utilize the land instead of letting the grass grow there. Having a home compost pile will also provide you with natural fertilizer. The weeding and watering can be reduced if you mulch the garden properly.

Landscaping with Food Giving Plants

You can beautify your garden and still produce food in it. Many plants provide beautiful visuals and also grow food that you and your family can consume. Growing such multi-tasking plants will work to your benefit. A lot of fruit trees that flower in the spring will also provide shade and keep your house cool in the summer. For a small yard, you can opt for dwarf varieties. You can start growing blackberry, raspberry, and other fruit-bearing bushes that add structure and also provide berries for years to come.

Instead of annual flowering plants, you should grow more produce plants. These can be practical and colorful additions to any garden. Scarlet runner beans grow quickly with edible pods and beautiful red flowers, while rhubarb plants have giant leaves and reddish-green stalks that are great too. You can also grow edible flower plants, such as nasturtiums or pansies that can be added to salads. Swiss chard is colorful and can be grown in hanging baskets. Under taller plants, you can cover the ground with smaller ones, such as strawberries and oregano.

Grow Produce That You Will Consume

Think of the kind of produce that you tend to consume more often. Growing these will make more sense than random plants when you have limited space. Think of the foods that you usually buy or eat a lot of and plan your garden accordingly. If you usually make smoothies in the morning, you can grow ingredients such as kale or strawberries for them. If you use lettuce and spinach for your salads, grow these in your garden. You might like some uncommon or expensive foods that set you back a pretty penny at the store, so try growing them instead.

Once in a while, review the output from your garden from a financial perspective. Consider the difference in cost between buying those products and growing or raising them yourself.

Growing expensive ingredients yourself will save you a lot of money on your grocery bills. However, certain foods are cheaper to buy than to grow. If a particular product is available at a very low price in your area, you don't have to spend your time and effort growing it. Instead, utilize the space to grow something else.

In this manner, you should evaluate your effort every season. Did some crops fail? Did you grow too much of something and too little of another? Using this information, you can make adjustments to your plan for the next season and invest your energy in the right way.

Plant Vertically

A lot of people fail to use the vertical space available in their backyard. Don't focus solely on using up the ground space. By planting a few crops vertically, you can grow more in less space. Consider adding vining plants such as peas, cucumbers, and pole beans to your garden, which can easily be supported by teepees or posts. You can also train sprawling plants such as melons and tomatoes to grow upright using trellises or heavy cages. It will take a little extra work to grow this way, but you will have more produce for it. Growing vertically also protects your plants from slugs and snails from the ground and fungal diseases. Just make sure that the plants get adequate water and light.

Utilize Rainwater

Rainwater is a great way to water your plants without wasting groundwater or spending too much money. Rain barrels can be installed under downspouts. The collected rainwater can be used for irrigating your garden for a while. You can buy commercially made barrels that are found in various sizes or materials. It is better to use a barrel with an overflow valve that keeps water away from your home once it reaches full capacity. The barrel should also have a spigot valve that can be connected to a hose for watering and a fine mesh screen that will keep insects out. Other than these commercial barrels, it is easy to make your own as well with some materials. However, before you start rainwater collection, check the regulations for your area. They might not permit installations of rain barrels. If this is the case, rainwater can still be utilized by growing plants such as watercress and chervil in spots where the water tends to collect after a storm.

Raise Bees and Other Small Farm Animals

If your backyard has enough space for a shed, coop, or a hive, you can try raising some animals or bees. Many residential areas allow you to raise small farm animals, honeybees, and fowl. You just have to check the ordinances in your zone and get the required permits or licenses. If you raise some chickens, you can have a supply of eggs and meat. Bird droppings can also be used for natural fertilization in the garden. If you want your own supply of milk, try raising a couple of goats. The Nigerian Dwarf variety can give you nearly three quarts every day. If you grow honeybees, you get a supply of honey and beeswax. The bees will also help to pollinate your garden. There are so many possibilities if you can make space for such animals in your yard.

Composting

You can make your own soil enhancements by having a compost bin. This way, you can turn any food scraps and garden trimmings into rich food for your plants. You can use the compost for adding nutrients to the soil, and this will improve the soil quality, thus promoting plant growth. The best part is that anyone can try composting because it just requires things such as leaves, clay soil, plant waste, or garden debris. When you add a layer of mulch over the soil, it will combat weeds and reduce the amount of water used. Organic mulch also improves soil quality once it decomposes. Grass clippings and fallen leaves from your own garden can be used for mulching.

Chapter Two: Considerations Before You Begin

Local zoning codes and ordinances should always be considered before planning any farm project or getting livestock. Another consideration is to determine how much time and money you have to invest in your project. What are your goals? Do you intend to have livestock? What structures will you need to build? Is there a water source available, or will you need to make a water catchment? What about a power source?

No matter how big or small your farm, you need to figure out a few things before you start. This will allow you to maximize the experience and reap the rewards of your efforts.

Time

The most important factor that everyone has to consider is time. Think before you commit to something that will take up more time than you can invest. Be realistic about the amount of time that you will be able to devote to the farm. Consider how much time all your other commitments take. Depending on the amount of time that you have available, you will be able to decide on the type of farm you grow.

Space

The time and space you have available are correlated. The more space there is for a farm, the more time it will require to build and maintain. If you have a large backyard and want to turn all of it into a mini farm, it will require a lot more time than you might imagine. If you have limited time available, decide on using a smaller space in the backyard, and increase the size later if time permits. The space you have available will also determine the types of plants you grow or the kind of livestock you can keep.

Water

Water is a crucial aspect of any farm. Does your backyard have easy access to water? This is especially important for those who live in dry climates. Will you have to pay for the water supply? Will you have to use hoses, or is there a sprinkler system? Will it be easy to repair if any issues arise with the water pipes? The watering methods used in a backyard farm are usually different from what is used in off-site farms. In your backyard farm, you will be more likely to use watering cans, soaker hoses, or drip lines. Weeds grow less frequently if the area between plants is not watered. If you use sprinklers, most of the ground will be watered, and this increases the chances of weeds. If you want to use sprinklers, you have a higher overhead delivery of water, more watering frequency, and there are problems such as fungus growth or powdery mildew.

Soil

The soil in your backyard has to be appropriate to grow all the plants you want. You have to check if your soil is ready to be used or will require a lot of improvement. Find out if the area was used for planting before. If not, then what else was done there? It is important for you to get a soil test done if you want to take this seriously. This will allow you to make the necessary adjustments and improvements to the soil to make it suitable for plant growth.

Sharing

It will be impossible to do every task on your farm alone, so you have to learn to share the load equally. Figure out a schedule and tasks for whoever is involved and assign the duties before the season begins. This will allow you to get the work done better and quicker. If you are sharing the space with someone else, then you have to figure out a way to work together harmoniously and without affecting the other's work.

Equipment

Do you have the necessary equipment for your farm, like hoses or other equipment? Make a list of what you have and what you will need to buy. Invest in some of the basic farm tools that everyone needs.

These are all the basic things that you have to consider while starting out.

Other than what is mentioned above, there are other things you have to keep in mind as well.

Learn About the Small Farm Business in Your Region

More than 95 percent of the farms in the U.S. are family-owned. This is why small farms are of major importance in the agricultural industry. A small farm is classified as such by the USDA Economic Research Service if it earns less than $350,000 in a year. The U.S. has nearly two million small farms, including retirement farms and off-farm occupation farms. You should look at the USDA website for more specifications to see if your farm will be considered a small farm business.

Consider Why You Want to Start Your Small Farm in the First Place

If you want to start a mini farm successfully, you need to understand your reasons for doing it first. Have clear intentions and goals for your mini farm. Is it just for self-sustainability? Is it because you want to make some money? Do you want to be more environmentally friendly? Your intention or motivation is what will impact most of your strategy. Think of such questions and be truthful with yourself to determine where you want to go with the small farm. It might be a hobby that ultimately turns into a small side business.

However, the tax implications will be different for a business farm as opposed to a hobby farm.

Get Some Real Experience

In the case of large farms, most skills and knowledge related to farming are passed down through generations. However, for a small-scale farmer or a beginner, it is important to acquire this knowledge themselves. Simply watching videos or reading books on it is not enough. You should talk to experienced farmers and get your hands dirty with real farming experience. This is the best way to become successful at growing plants or raising livestock. Learning from others will also help you avoid the mistakes they initially made and understand the various risks associated with farming. If you want to make a profit from your small farm, you should also get the business know-how that will help you with it. You only have to put in a little time and effort to do all this.

Learn as You Go

You may never have farmed before, but once you set your mind to it, anyone can do it. You can start with a few plants and learn how to get better at growing more. Farming is a little more large scale than growing a few herbs in your garden. However, if you can do the latter, you can slowly move forward into growing your farm too. The best part about farming is that you can keep learning as you go. The more you do and communicate with other farmers, the better you get at it. Using a guide such as this book helps you to fast track your way toward having a successful small farm. But the most important thing is to put everything you learn to practical use. Your skills will be honed as you keep working. The more you learn, the more confidently you can expand your growing area each season. It is best to start small and go from there.

Decide if Your Mini Farm is a Hobby or a Business

If you want to start your farm purely out of interest or to be self-sustainable, keep it as a hobby farm. This allows you to experiment a lot more and enjoy the whole experience of farming. If you have adequate space and want to make some money from your efforts, then you can turn it into a business farm. But you need to decide what you want from the beginning in order to plan and execute accordingly.

Do Your Market Research

You should not skip the phase of market research, as it's an important step for someone who wants to turn their mini farm into a business. If you have decided what you want to grow and raise on your farm, you should do the market research accordingly. You will need to find out who your potential customers are and where you will be selling your products. You have to figure out a plan for doing all of it while keeping competitors in mind. It is not very difficult to carry out some informal market research even if you haven't done it before. Learn more about the local market, farmer's market, et cetera. Also, check if certain produce is under-represented at these places so you can provide the supply. The local state agricultural department will be of assistance during this phase of research. You will also be able to learn what license you need and the guidelines for food safety and market access.

Getting Financed

If you don't have enough money to start the farm, you have to consider options to get financed. There are a few ways that you can finance your farm without being knee-deep in debt. Taking out a loan with your credit card is one of the options that you should not opt for. There are other ways, like self-financing, which will allow you to make profits and not be worried about debt. It is also important to be realistic in the beginning. Don't aim to buy expensive equipment with a loan right at the beginning. Instead, you need to get the basics and slowly build on these. If your business takes off, you can start buying what you need to make the farm run more smoothly. Running a profitable operation on a small budget will also make it easier for you to get a larger loan from banks later.

Market and Sell

You can market and sell your farm products in many ways. The most obvious way to do so is at the local farmers market. There are other channels that you can consider, as well. You can even set up a farm shop or produce stand on your property if it is big enough and there is a lot of traffic there. Another option is through Community Support Agriculture, when a share of your yield will be purchased by the patron for a fixed price regularly, whenever produce is ready. You can also sell with other local growers under a united brand. Some food stores might also be willing to sell your produce as well, so make sure you approach them. Assess your options and put a marketing plan together.

Chapter Three: Creating a Layout for Your Space

Now let's get into the subject of a mini farm layout—creating a blueprint design to fit the yard's dimensions, designating grow spaces, water catchment, composting, tool storage, and workspace will pay large dividends. You also have to prepare a seasonal calendar that maps the time for planting seeds indoors, harvest schedules, crop rotation, et cetera.

It can be really fun to brainstorm ideas and create a layout for your new mini farm. However, it can also be challenging. You may be a beginner or already have some experience with gardening and raising animals, but you still need to keep some basics in mind.

When you begin, it can be quite easy to get carried away. You may be excited, but jumping right into running a mini farm without giving it some thought can do more harm than good. It takes careful planning, organizing, and time to be successful at running a farm.

First, you have to figure out your goals, both long term and short term. These goals will help you decide how to get started with gardening and what animals to raise. You may want to insert a greenhouse on your farm later, so you need to plan out an area where it can go. If you set goals for the future as well, it allows you to plan ahead and have a smooth transition later. Your goals will help you map out the yard appropriately. Making a list of the large-scale projects will help you to design them in advance and to plan a budget.

Before you start designing the layout, keep these things in mind:

• You have to check the zoning laws in your area for gardening and animals. This is especially important in urban areas. The laws often require you to maintain a certain distance from your neighbor's land. There are also regulations about the animals you may or may not be allowed to keep. Certain areas don't permit a garden in the front yard as well. Some areas have rules about keeping a specific number of animals and housing them a certain distance away from the neighbor's house. It is easy to look up the provincial and state laws in your location.

• You also have to keep the sunlight exposure in different parts of the yard in mind. Plants such as corn or tomatoes will need more than eight hours of direct sunlight in a day. Other plants, such as leafy greens, will only need four to six hours of sun exposure. You have to observe the light falling on your yard to determine where you should plant your crops accordingly. You also have to keep the shadows from trees or buildings in perspective. If you are building structures such as greenhouses or sheds, you can grow shade friendly plants around them.

• If you are adding animals to your backyard farm, think of everything you will need. Plan out the building you will house them in. You might need to have an area for feeding or keeping hay. If you want to start with a few animals and add more at a later time, you will need to ensure that you have enough space to do that in your layout. Plan the structure in a way that you can build on later without affecting the garden around it.

• Fencing is another major factor to be considered. If your area has animals such as elk or bears around, you need a fence big enough to keep them out. Rodents are common in urban areas, so your fencing has to be done accordingly. The costs of building the farm add up when you have to add large fencing around the yard to protect the garden and animals.

- If you want to plant bushes and trees, you need to place them in areas where they won't cast a shadow over your plants. Planting these can be expensive, but they are worth it in the long run. You have to consider the space the tree will take up when it grows as well. If you have limited space, you can look up trees that take less space and plant these. There are dwarf varieties of many fruit trees that you can try growing too.

Mapping Out the Yard

After considering the above-mentioned points, budget, and land restrictions, you can start designing the farm. Regardless of how small or big your yard is, you have to map it out. It could be a large acreage or even a small lot in an urban area. Taking your goals into consideration, you can draw and design a few different options for your yard. Doodling many different combinations for the layout will help you figure out the best one in the end. Your plans will probably change according to your budget and with time.

If you want to focus more on gardening, then having a garden planner will be helpful. Create a plan to map where you will grow certain plants and the square footage you want to allow for them. You need to specify space for every structure you intend to build, the machinery you might need, tool storage, et cetera. This will make the process of maintaining and working on the farm more seamless and efficient.

The following tips will help you to create a layout for your farm:

1. Arrange everything in the most efficient way possible for your farm.

2. The planning should be done in a way that also reduces labor costs.

3. Choose the system of farming first and then create the layout of the farm. The layout will be different according to the type of farming system you will follow.

4. Efficient space utilization is essential. You will only have a certain amount of space to work with, so it needs to be used in the ideal way possible. Wasting space will not work in your favor.

5. Accessibility is another factor. You should be able to access everything on the farm easily without any hindrances. You have to keep adequate space between the plant beds, equipment, structures, et cetera, so that you can move around freely. The layout of the farm should facilitate the easy handling of materials and equipment, and the design should allow the work to be done with the minimum movement required. Everything should be directly accessible.

6. Visibility is also important so that there is proper lighting, and everything can be overseen conveniently.

Creating a Seasonal Calendar

Having a seasonal calendar will play a big role in your homestead. Just like you map out the layout of the farm, you should also make a plan for when certain things will have to be done through the year. As a beginner, you will make a lot of mistakes, but with careful planning, you can avoid a lot of them as well.

One thing to remember is that you cannot do everything at the same time. Your farm may be in your backyard, but there are other obligations you have in life as well. You have to plan things out in a way that is convenient and realistic. Don't try to get everything done at the same time. You also don't have to try and do everything others are doing on their farms. There are many different things you can try out over time and see what works best for you. You don't have to raise chickens and pigs and bees at the same time.

Over time, see what works best and stick to that in the long run. Think of what will benefit you and your family the most while working on your garden. Don't grow food that no one in your house likes to eat. Don't raise animals that are more work than you can handle. Just find what fits your needs and budget and work on that. Another point is that you should use the seasons as a guide. You can divide your work better through the year if you follow the seasons.

Grow things in the season that they usually perform best in. This will reduce your workload and help your plants grow well. Instead of trying to grow out of season plants that require a lot of care, grow ones that will naturally flourish in your garden with minimal effort on your part. Timing is very important when raising plants and animals. You should learn more about gardening calendars and vaccination schedules for livestock as well.

Every person's farm is different, and what you do in yours will depend entirely on you. You can create a seasonal calendar purely for your own farm, while using others as a guide. No one can dictate what you should grow, when, or how much. You have to figure all this out yourself as you work on the farm. Having a plan will just help you to carry things out more smoothly through the year.

Chapter Four: Building Your Needed Structures

To start a proper farm, you have to consider building the various structures required, as it will ensure your mini farm success. Structures to consider are sheds for food and tool storage, chicken coops, compost bins, workstations, greenhouses, and hoop houses. You can save money by re-purposing things for these projects. Here you will learn how to build a few of the structures that are common on farms.

Building a Shed

It can be extremely rewarding to build your own shed, even though it is a bit challenging.

Here's how you can build your shed in the backyard:

Get a Permit

Find out about the building codes in your locality. Some areas require you to get a building permit before you build a shed in your yard. You can ask the building office and enquire about the specifics. They will tell you how you can get your hands on a permit and start on your shed. Don't take the risk of building the shed before getting the permit because your hard work might entirely go to waste. If the permit is not granted, the whole shed will have to be torn down. You have to learn about the local building codes, so the shed is approved by the authorities.

Leveling

The ground may have to be leveled, and you need to install some deck piers that will support the shed. Deck piers allow you to string the support beams below the shed floor. For instance, in one direction, you can place the piers about six feet apart, and in another direction, you can place them four feet apart. This will allow the whole grid area to be about twelve x eight feet. It is convenient to follow this because you will only need three plywood sheets of four x eight feet to cover it once you lay the supports along the grid. If you want to build the shed on a slab of concrete, it is important to lay the concrete slab before building the shed. The concrete will help to protect the shed from any water that seeps in from the soil. Following shed plans will make it easier to build. You can create the plan yourself or download a pre-planned professional option.

Support Beams

Support beams should be strung across the deck piers in a lengthwise manner. It will support the floor joists running in the opposite direction. Metal straps are the easiest way to attach the beams to piers. These metal straps have built-in nail holes.

Joists are to be attached to support beams and separated with blocking. A rim joist has to be attached along the outermost edge of every outer support beam. The rim joists have to be of the same length as the beams below them. Then floor joists will have to be installed across the whole length of your support beams. The length of the floor joists has to be such that they fit between two rim joists. Installing a piece of blocking between every two-floor joists along the support beam in the center will prevent the floor joists from moving.

Floor

For the floor of the shed, plywood sheeting has to be nailed to the joists. Along with nailing the sheets, you can also use H-clips that fit between a pair of plywood pieces and add structural strength by locking them together. You can also screw down the shed floor with 3-inch deck screws.

Framework

The framework for the four walls has to be built. The front walls are different from the back walls, and the sidewalls have to be sloped, so all of these should be tackled separately. It will be easier to do the back wall first and then the front followed by the sidewalls. To build the back-wall framework, the bottom and top beams should be of the same length as that of the floor where they will sit. If you keep the spacing between the floor-joists the same as the spacing between the vertical studs, it will keep the measurements simple.

The front wall should be higher than the back wall, as this will allow the roof to slow and direct rainwater away from the door. To build the front wall framework, make sure that it is the same as the back wall but taller. It should have a doorframe too so that you can add a door to the shed later. To build the sidewall framework, make sure that the bottom plates are of the length that will allow the sidewalls to fit between the front and back wall. In the US, the standard spacing is 16 inches between vertical wall studs. The top plate has to be angled to make the roof sloped. This means that the vertical studs will have different heights. Then all the wall structures have to be assembled and nailed from the bottom up to the underlying support. You can also nail them through the joists and plywood. You will need some help when you do this, as someone needs to hold the wall structures up while they are joined.

1. Rafters have to be built across the roof and separated with blocking. The rafters will overhang the walls as they provide more weather protection. Keep the rafter spacing the same as the floor joist spacing so that your measurements are simple. Then attach the blocking between every pair of rafters on the top plates.

2. The roof can be formed by nailing plywood sheets on the rafters. The plywood layout for the floor will have to be altered if you add an overhang.

3. The walls will have to be covered by materials such as textured plywood or siding to give it a finished look.

4. Adding tarpaper in overlapping layers on the roof will protect the shed from having rainwater seeping through the cracks.

Building a Greenhouse

Having a greenhouse in your backyard will allow you to grow a variety of plants all through the year. It allows the farmer or gardener to create a perfect environment for their plants. You can get a head start on your spring planting, and the growing season can be extended beyond autumn. While traditional greenhouses can be expensive, there are other cheaper options too. You can buy a greenhouse kit that is ready to be assembled. You can also choose to build a greenhouse from scratch in your backyard.

Before you decide on the right greenhouse for your farm, you have to consider a few factors:

Ordinances

Before you start building a greenhouse, check the rules in your area to see if you are even allowed to do so. You will probably have to apply for a permit, since greenhouses are usually considered outbuildings. If your community has a homeowner's association, you will need their approval as well. This can prove difficult in many communities because their housing policies are usually against outbuildings. This is why it is important to learn of the ordinances before you even plan your greenhouse.

Sunlight

The orientation of the sun is another important factor. Greenhouses are built to provide plants with a sunny and warm environment optimal for their growth. The location of the greenhouse in your backyard is important. Optimally, the greenhouse should face south or southeast. This will allow it to capture light from the early morning sun. In most climates, an east-facing greenhouse works well too. You should build the greenhouse in a place where it will receive uninterrupted sunlight for at least six hours in the day. If your region experiences heavy snowfall, you should also ensure that the greenhouse would be able to support the snow load without collapsing.

Glazing

Traditionally glass is used as a glazing material for a greenhouse. However, glass can be expensive, fragile, and heavy. This is why DIY greenhouses usually use materials such as acrylic, polycarbonate, polyethylene sheeting, or fiberglass for glazing. Acrylic, fiberglass, and polycarbonate sheets are good insulators, resilient, and allow great light transmission. However, fiberglass tends to get discolored with time. Polyethylene sheets are very affordable and can be easy to install. However, they are not tough and get damaged quite easily.

Framing

The frames of most greenhouses are made with metal or wood. For small or medium-sized greenhouses, wood can be a cheaper option and is easier to work with. Metal is more costly than wood but is stronger and has better resistance to weather. Aluminum is a great option because it is strong, lightweight, and resistant to corrosion.

Flooring

The floor material of a greenhouse can be gravel, flagstone, wood decking, poured concrete, metal grates, or even bare dirt. However, a bare dirt floor is only efficient if the yard is usually bone dry. If not, it will be a muddy mess inside the greenhouse. Concrete is a durable option but does not drain well and is expensive. Gravel drains well and is relatively inexpensive. You can also refurbish gravel floors easily just by adding more.

Temperature Regulation

It is critical to be able to regulate temperatures inside greenhouses, because winters can be too cold, and summers can get too hot for the plants. Having exhaust fans, operable windows, or rooftop vents will help you to expel the hot air from your greenhouse. Shade cloths can be used for blocking solar heat too. When it is bitterly cold, an electric heater can be installed to keep the greenhouse warm. Use one that has a fan that can be thermostatically controlled. If the climate in your region is moderate, the cold can be chased away with passive solar systems. You can also try stacking concrete blocks or barrels filled with water inside the greenhouse. These will absorb the energy from the sun in the day and then release the heat at night when the temperature drops.

Building an Outdoor Compost Bin

Compost allows you to improve the fertility of your soil, nourish helpful microbes, carry out moisture management, and protect the soil from harmful microbes. Creating a three-bin system will help you to pump out a lot of useful compost within weeks. If you approach composting in a more hands-off way, it will take months to get any rich compost for use in the garden. Using cedar that is rot-resistant will allow you to have a great, long-lasting compost bin, compared to others.

Working the Compost Bin

You can use compostable substances such as vegetable and fruit scraps, dry leaves, old newspapers, and wood-shavings to fill one compost bin. Once this bin is full, the contents should be turned into the second bin. You should turn the contents of the bin every couple of days as this promotes faster decomposition. So, the more you turn, the more decomposition occurs. Then start filling the third bin with fresh compostable material. When this bin is full, the compost in the second bin is done, and the first one is empty, you can start composting from the beginning all over again.

Building a Chicken Coop

If you want to raise chickens on your farm, you need a chicken coop. While you can buy a pre-fabricated one, building one yourself might be fun and cheaper. If you have some basic skills in woodworking, it is fairly simple to build a chicken coop. However, you need to plan it out properly if you don't have any previous experience in it.

Decide How Big or Small You Want the Coop to Be

The size of your chicken coop has to be determined before all other work. Generally, each chicken requires about three square feet of space in a coop. So, depending on how many chickens you want to raise, you have to consider the footage of the coop. If you want to keep four chickens, then you need a coop of at least twelve square feet. However, if you plan on keeping the chickens inside the coop all the time, each chicken should have eight to ten square feet of space. Having a cramped-up coop will stress out the chickens, make them sick, and could cause them to die. The coop itself will get dirty very fast and smell bad. It is okay to keep three square feet of space per chicken only if you allow them outside most of the time. The bantam breed chickens need even less space.

Decide Where You Will Place the Coop

The location of the coop is the second factor you need to consider. You have to place it somewhere that gets natural sunlight in the daytime. There should be good airflow as well, but not too much exposure to strong winds. Placing the coop below the shade of a large tree can take care of the sun, shade, and wind factors. You should also ensure ease of access, as the coop needs to be checked a couple of times each day. So, place it somewhere that makes it easy for you to check on the chickens. The chicken coop can be noisy and smelly as well, so keep it at an appropriate distance from your house or of any neighbors. You can monitor your backyard for a few days to decide the right location for the coop.

Now You Can Start Planning the Coop

A coop is not just a roof and four walls to keep the chickens protected. It is a space that keeps your chickens healthy and alive. You have to add a nesting box for the chickens to lay eggs in. One box is enough for two hens. These should be about ten inches above the ground and be around twelve x twelve x twelve inches in size. The coop should have proper light and ventilation, or the chickens can easily get sick. You also have to add feeders and waterers for the chickens to eat and drink from. While these are the basics, you should also consider other additions to the coop. A perch area is great for chickens, as they love sleeping on the perch. Have a fenced outdoor area in the backyard for them to play. A dust bath box will allow the chickens to clean themselves and stay healthy. Having a poop board below the perching area will save you time while cleaning. Add lighting to the coop for winters; it will boost the production of eggs.

Once you have planned out and got everything ready, you can start building the chicken coop. There are plenty of plans available on the Internet or in books. You can use the instructions for the shed mentioned above and modify it accordingly.

These are some of the structures that you should consider building in your backyard to turn it into an efficient mini farm.

Chapter Five: Getting Started Growing Organic

The trend of organic gardening has prompted a lot of gardeners and beginners to switch to alternative and DIY gardening methods. In agriculture and general gardening, organic means anything that is grown without the use of any synthetic fertilizers, artificial hormones, or pesticides.

Scientifically speaking, organic gardening is described as an ecological production management technique that promotes soil biological activity, biodiversity, and biological cycles. Organic gardening practices promote and enhance natural biodiversity, and focus on making the garden and the gardener self-sufficient and sustainable. If you are a newbie who is just beginning their organic gardening experience, here are a few tips for you:

Use Organic Garden Soil or Mulch

To grow organic and healthy fruits and vegetables, you have to start with healthy and fertile soil. Organic matter is the most important component of soil. Using organic matter such as compost, peat moss, or manure can improve the quality of the plants. Manure and mulch contain decaying matter that is left-over from the previous plant cycles. These microorganisms supply plants with the nutrients that they need.

You can make your compost by using a bin or a designated area where you dispose of the organic waste from your kitchen.

If the process seems too lengthy and troublesome, you can purchase it from suppliers, garden centers, and home-improvement stores. Spreading a one inch thick layer of mulch on your garden bed can reduce the growth of weeds and other unwanted plants. Mulching also prevents any spores containing fungal diseases from drifting onto the plants and ruining them. Mulch is made of organic materials such as straw, cocoa hulls, and newspapers. The mulch decomposes over time and adds beneficial organic matter into the soil.

Use Organic Gardening Fertilizers

Fertilizing vegetables and fruits is necessary if you want your plants to grow faster and yield better produce. Organic farming means that you have to use organic fertilizers, such as manure from animals (for example: cows, chickens, rabbits, or goats). If you have no access to animal manure or decomposing compost, you can order prepackaged organic fertilizers from Amazon or other online stores. You can find a range of different organic fertilizers in flower shops and home-improvement stores. You can skip using fertilizers if you already have nutrient-rich soil. Over-fertilized soil can make your plants soft and prone to pest and disease infestations.

Shopping for Seedlings

When you are buying seedlings, a lot of horticulturists recommend using plants that exhibit healthy colors, with an absence of yellow or withered leaves. Avoid buying saplings or seedlings that have droopy or wilting leaves. When you are buying transplants (saplings that are semi-grown and need to be transplanted into the garden), remove them out of the pots, and examine their roots to make sure that they are healthy. You want to buy saplings that have white, well-developed roots. Avoid buying plants that have already formed buds or flowers. If you cannot avoid buying them, remove the buds and flowers using gardening scissors. This allows the plant to utilize all its energy on setting new roots instead of diverting essential resources into the buds and flowers.

Crop Rotation

Many plants and crops are affected by seasonal diseases and crop infestations. You can tackle this problem by planting these crops and avoiding the spots where their diseased ancestors were growing. Two plants that have a common history for facing this problem are tomatoes (including eggplants, potatoes, tomatoes, and peppers) and squash (including squash pumpkin, watermelon, and cucumber). Rotating these crops to different parts of your garden after every harvest can help to prevent disease infestations and avoid the complete depletion of nutrients in the soil.

Maintenance and Picking Weeds

Weeds can be pesky, and they can overrun your garden within a few days. If you are serious about organic gardening, get ready for some daily weeding. Although many herbicides and weedicides are effective in killing these unwanted plants, they can also make the soil toxic, killing things that are beneficial for the soil. The only effective method to avoid this is to pull them out by hand. Pulling weeds is easier when the soil is wet and muddy, so you're better off doing it after it has rained or after you water your garden. You can pull out the roots by gently pinching the base of the stem, or you can use a weeding trowel if you are removing larger bits of vegetation. It might take you a while before you are comfortable doing it properly, so be careful not to damage the plants while you are getting the hang of it.

Keeping your garden clean is very important, especially if you want your plants to grow well. You should develop a habit of walking through your garden and picking up any dead foliage once a week. Picking off one infected leaf prevents a disease from spreading throughout your organic plant garden.

Producing your vegetables, fruits, or herbs organically is a long-term process and better carried out in different stages, instead of one single change adopted in a short time. Adopting organic gardening techniques means that you will have to transition from your conventional lifestyle into an organic one.

The first step of the process is having good quality and quantity of soil where you can grow your organic garden. If you already have a small backyard or garden, you can assign a small area for your organic gardening purposes and improve the soil fertility and soil quality in that area. Although soil is non-sentient and non-living, it is a very dynamic resource and biologically active in terms of the different microbes and chemical reactions that happen in it. It provides every plant with the water, mineral nutrients, and oxygen that it needs to grow.

Not having to rely on someone else for food and having an environment-friendly garden is a win-win. You have your very own source of delicious and chemical-free organic food, and the surrounding environment gets the necessary protection and resources that it needs. The best aspect of organic gardening is that it is an easy process. There are a lot of benefits to having your organic garden.

Not only is it a great way to reduce your carbon footprint and eat chemical-free food, you and your family will also be happy knowing that the food that you are eating is organic and healthy for you. Aside from the tasty organic produce, organic gardening also saves you a lot of money and gives you a way of spending your free time in a productive and fulfilling way. In this chapter, we will be digging deeper into the different benefits that organic gardening has to offer.

Benefits of Organic Gardening

Health Benefits

Since organic gardening practices completely eliminate the use of synthetic chemical pesticides and fertilizers, you will be handling no chemicals. This means no spraying toxic chemicals and injecting artificial growth hormones, which is what happens in most large-scale agriculture practices. You will be reducing the overall nitrate content in your food when you are not using any synthetic nitrate-based fertilizers.

No Toxins

Most mass-produced vegetables or fruits are grown using a lot of cancer-causing pesticides/insecticides and unnatural genetic modifications. Some of these chemicals are still on the surfaces, even if you wash them with water. Surveys have shown that a large part of the population in countries such as India, Japan, and the USA have DDT, mercury, and other harmful chemicals in their bodies. These toxic chemicals can cause systemic and life-threatening diseases.

High Nutrition

Organically grown food has proven to be better for your health compared to any mass grown produce. It delivers more antioxidants, higher nutrient content, and can improve your overall health. The biggest factor that contributes to better health is that your tendency to eat veggies and fruits increases, because you have access to tasty and healthy food that you've grown yourself.

No GMO Food

Organic gardening eliminates the need for consuming GMOs (genetically modified organisms). GMOs are plants that are artificially bred in order to exhibit certain characteristics. These plants have had their most fundamental blueprint of life altered and mixed in with other species of plants and animals. For instance, fish DNA is implanted into tomatoes to make them disease resistant, bacterial DNA is implanted into corn to increase the output of the crop, and spider DNA is injected into goats to increase the production of milk. Although these genetic modifications may improve the crop by making it resistant to different diseases and pests, it is not healthy because the human body is not adapted to ingest and process these GMOs. There are a few cases where GMO foods were nearly disastrous for human health. Organic produce is not genetically modified in any way whatsoever. By law, you cannot genetically modify organic seeds.

Saving Money

Having your organic garden and growing your own vegetables can save you a lot of money if you do it right, and that is something that everybody likes. When you follow organic gardening practices, you will be spending a lot less on gardening supplies such as fertilizers and chemical pesticides. Instead of spending money on these things, organic gardening encourages the use of food scraps, kitchen waste, and yard clippings. Not only do they act as natural fertilizers that are free of toxic chemicals, but they also help the environment by replenishing nutrients and microbes in the soil.

Most people aren't aware of the fact that they can easily make insecticides or herbicides from things that are found in every kitchen. Growing your own organic produce instead of purchasing it from the supermarket or the farmer's market can save you up to 50% of your normal expenditure. Not only do you reduce your expenses at the grocery store, but you also avoid transportation costs and packaging costs as well. You can also ensure that your food supply remains unaffected during the winter months by preserving and storing your produce. You can even grow bumper crops during these off seasons and avoid the need to buy greenhouse-raised produce.

Environmental Benefits

No Chemicals

As the name suggests, organic gardening involves the use of organic insecticides and fertilizers instead of toxic chemical-based substitutes. You may come across some studies on the Internet, which appear to "show" the benefits of chemically grown food, but they are likely to have been funded by the pesticide industry. It is a fact that nitrate-rich fertilizers can kill earthworms, causing serious damage to natural soil ecology and contaminating the food with cell-damaging nitrates. The chemical fertilizers and pesticides that are used in large-scale agricultural practices produce field runoff, which can contaminate the soil and water sources.

Growing crops organically is eco-friendly because the plants are allowed to grow just as nature intended. The lack of fungicides, pesticides, herbicides, and fertilizers (which are poisons) reduce the pollution of water sources and the soil.

Good for the Soil

Growing your vegetables or fruits without the use of toxic fertilizers or insecticides is healthier for the plant and the soil. Crops grown without herbicides or pesticides are more colorful, tastier, and healthier than non-organic crops. This is due to the use of nutrient-dense soil instead of synthetic chemicals. Organically grown fruits and vegetables are much tastier because they are given more time to grow and mature.

The chemical-based fertilizers, pesticides, fungicides, and herbicides that are used in large-scale agricultural practices are indiscriminate, killing all of the beneficial and non-beneficial organisms, such as garden critters, earthworms, and microbes. These chemicals ruin the biodiversity of the soil, and the crops that are subsequently grown tend to become weaker and prone to diseases. When you practice organic gardening, you are not using these toxic chemicals to make your plants grow, which means that your soil becomes nutrient-rich, and the plants grow better. Preserving the biodiversity of your garden soil directly correlates to better plant health.

Good Returns and Low Carbon Footprint

If organic farming is carried out on a large scale (community organic farming), the organically grown produce will be sold locally within the same community. This can reduce the carbon footprint of the entire community, which benefits the environment.

Pest Resistant

You may have the notion that organically grown plants are more vulnerable to diseases and pests, since no pesticides or chemicals are used, but the opposite is true. Organically grown vegetables and fruits are more resistant to pests and diseases. Since these plants have sufficient time to develop and grow, they develop an inherent resistance to certain diseases naturally. The plants are grown in nutrient-rich soil, and this allows the plant to become much healthier, increasing its chances of surviving infestations and diseases.

Organic Farming and Sustainable Development

In a study conducted by Columbia University of New York, it was found that food production systems and supply chains were one of the largest contributors to the degradation of the environment.

The production, transportation, and consumption of food on a planet as large as ours, containing more than seven billion people, is a very carbon-intensive process. Agricultural activities account for up to one-third of global greenhouse gas emissions (GHG emissions), mainly due to the process of land conversion and loss of forest cover.

With the global food output expected to double by the year 2050, things look grim. The ongoing climate change crisis requires us to take a look beyond the conventional systems of food production and come up with more sustainable ways of feeding the human population.

Organic farming adopts natural approaches and the use of organic fertilizers and manure, crop rotation, and other sustainable practices. This reduces the exposure of growers and consumers to chemicals that are harmful to them and the environment as well. When used without control, pesticides and fertilizers can create a host of environmental problems. These pesticides can poison the soil and kill non-target organisms such as worms, birds, rodents, and fish. Organisms such as bees and algae, which are ecologically important, can also get harmed by unsustainable farming practices.

Pesticides and fertilizers also contaminate the soil and the water table (groundwater). A study conducted by the United States Geological Service found that more than 90% of the water and fish samples that were collected were contaminated by pesticides. Fertilizers that seep into the water sources (streams, aquifers) can cause eutrophication or algal blooms. These algae hijack resources such as oxygen and nitrogen, creating dead zones with low oxygen content. These dead zones can kill marine life and disrupt the ecosystem. Since organic gardening does not involve the use of these harmful pesticides and fertilizers, it becomes a very sustainable form of agriculture in many aspects. Organic gardens tend to have more nutrient-rich and fertile soil, and these gardens also consume less energy, thereby reducing the carbon footprint. Research studies have shown that organic farms use 45% less energy as compared to conventional farms. Their carbon emissions are 40% lower than traditional farms, and these organic gardens foster 30% more biodiversity, compared to conventional farming gardens.

Drawbacks to Organic Farming

This being said, organic farming does have its drawbacks and might not prove to be sustainable in certain cases. For instance, a popular form of pest control without the use of chemical pesticides is laying down sheets of black tarp or plastic over the soil surrounding the crops. The cover warms up the soil and speeds up the growth of the plants while also preventing soil erosion.

The black tarpaulin also permits the usage of drip irrigation, which lets water slowly drip into the root of the plants, thereby saving water. However, the single big drawback to this is the sheer amount of plastic waste that is created, especially if the farming is done on a large scale. This is partially taken care of with the introduction of biodegradable plastic, which provides a more sustainable alternative. The problem isn't completely solved yet because these biodegradable plastics contain petroleum, which might pose its own set of problems to the environment.

Since organic farming does not allow the use of synthetic pesticides and fertilizers, the crop yield is 25% lower compared to conventional farming techniques. Instead, organic farming practices rely on activities such as tilling (running blades through the soil to kill weeds and unwanted vegetation). These activities can cause a gradual loss of the topsoil, reducing fertility and lowering the yields.

In a world that has an exponentially growing population and finite arable land, optimizing the resources that are available to us is essential for the continuity of life on Earth and human civilization. Organic farming on a larger scale also calls for a higher demand for agricultural land, the incentivization of deforestation and loss of habitat for wildlife and local fauna. This can threaten the biodiversity of the region and increase the overall carbon footprint.

Just because something is labeled "organic" does not necessarily mean that it is better or more sustainable. Organic farming does not work overnight; it requires a slow transition with the systematic replacement of conventional agricultural practices with sustainable ones. For instance, obtaining the necessary certification from the local authorities can be a highly bureaucratic process and extremely expensive in terms of money. These permits are designed to act as barriers for small-scale organic farmers and promote the use of synthetic chemical-based fertilizers and pesticides. Local health authorities or other governing bodies also mandate food to be wrapped in plastic, which goes against organic farming practices.

Chapter Six: Chickens, Bees, and Livestock

Creating your very own food supply is one of the best things that you can do for yourself. If you are planning to rely on yourself to procure your food supply, you will find some useful suggestions, and you can use this information to decide which animals are the right fit for you.

Just keep in mind that if you are looking to produce meat and dairy to sell, you will require a license, and your farm/homestead must also meet the requirements of the local health and sanitation department. Depending on how much land/space you have at your disposal, you can rear a number of different animals in order to meet your food requirements. Some of the common farm animals that you can raise are chickens, honeybees, goats, sheep, turkeys, rabbits, and ducks.

Chickens

Chickens are the best place to start when raising animals on a small farm or backyard because of the ease with which you can raise them. They are small, resilient, and very easy to take care of in terms of effort and attention required. Even the initial setup does not cost much, so it won't be making that big of a dent in your wallet. A family's requirement for eggs can easily be met by raising a small flock of chickens. Depending on how many chickens there are in a flock, you can get between five to ten eggs on a daily basis, which is sometimes more than what you will need. In fact, a flock of two or three-dozen chickens can easily generate enough eggs for one to start a little egg business.

Chickens are also one of the best ways of getting rid of food scraps and organic leftovers. They eat these food scraps and produce an extremely good fertilizer/compost with their excrement and chicken litter. The litter can be used for fertilizing plants and improving the output of your vegetable garden. The only downside of raising chickens is the free chicken dinner that you might be leaving for any predators that are lingering around. Since chickens are defenseless and easily slaughtered, you need to create safe enclosures and keep them secure to prevent any losses.

Raising chickens is an excellent activity if you have a lot of free time at your disposal. It can be therapeutic, fun, and rewarding for beginners and, at times, may even turn out to be nerve-wracking. The Internet can provide tons of information to raise chicks and chickens. Sorting through this information may sometimes become a difficult thing to do. It can be tricky to determine what is correct and what is not, but this book will help you with that information.

Choosing the Right Breed of Chicken

With the advent of scientific advancements and improvements in farming methods, we now have a stunning array of chickens to choose from. There are hundreds of different breeds of chickens, and although some of them may seem indiscernible from each other, every breed is slightly different. For instance, certain breeds may lay more eggs on average, some of them produce meat of higher quality, and some of them may be characterized by their distinct plumage. There are four different categories of chicken breeds:

Heritage Breeds

A heritage chicken is defined as a natural breeding chicken that has a slow growth rate and a long life span. Chickens belonging to this breed live a long and productive outdoor life.

Egg Laying Breeds

These breeds of chickens are specifically bred for the purpose of producing a large number of eggs through a short production lifetime. Leghorns and Australorps are the best examples of egg-laying breeds.

Dual Purpose Breeds

These breeds of chickens have the best qualities of the egg-laying breeds and the meat-producing breeds. They are highly productive and can produce a large number of eggs, and they can also grow large enough to produce a significant amount of meat at the later stages of their lives.

Meat Breeds

As the name aptly suggests, these breeds of chickens are specifically raised for the purpose of producing meat. They have a shorter life span and can grow very quickly. They gain body weight at a very fast pace and are big enough for slaughter after approximately nine to ten weeks.

When it comes to choosing a breed, you have to consider what you are looking to get out of your flock. For instance, if you are looking to get a lot of eggs and purchase a bunch of Sultan chicks—a heritage breed—you might be in for some disappointment.

How Many Chickens Should I Keep?

Chickens are birds that live in a flock, so you should start with two to three chickens if it is your very first time raising them. An adult hen lays two to three eggs every three days so you will have a steady supply of eggs if you start with two to three fowls. Chickens have the highest productivity in the first two to three years of their lives, and the egg-laying capacity gradually slows down after that. You will need to consider replacing your flock with new birds eventually. You can purchase new chicks from suppliers, or if you want to make things more interesting, you can even hatch your eggs if you have a rooster in your flock. However, this has a fairly low success rate, so I do not recommend doing this, especially if you have no prior experience.

How Much Space Do Chickens Require?

This will depend upon the number of chickens and the breed that you're raising. An experiment conducted by the University of Missouri Extension found that a medium-sized chicken requires at least three square feet of floor space inside the chicken coop, and eight to ten square feet of space outdoors. Your flock of chickens will be healthier and happier if they have more space, and the production of meat and eggs will be higher. Overcrowding and a lack of space contributes to feather picking and the spread of diseases.

A chicken requires space to spread its wings, so you will need a considerably big space if you are looking to raise chickens. This allows them to spend enough time outdoors, taking dust baths and feeding on worms and insects. Since chickens are small and defenseless creatures, you must create safe enclosures to prevent them from getting preyed on by predators (these predators include not only wild animals but also your pets, such as dogs and cats). You can add chicken wiring to your list of required equipment.

Cost of Operation

A major portion of the cost of production includes the starting cost of materials that are required to construct the chicken coop and an average twenty x five square feet chicken run. The raw materials that are required include wood, chicken fencing wires, and other hardware. All of these may set you back by a few bucks, but you will eventually break even and make up for the cost of production, when your expenditure for meat and eggs decreases. If you are not experienced at construction work, you will also need to hire someone to do it for you. Overall, the average starting cost can range between $500 and $700, depending upon the size of your flock and of the chicken coop.

Chickens and Gardening

Although chickens are primarily raised to produce eggs or for meat supply, they also happen to be one of the most helpful gardeners. Yes, chickens are extremely beneficial for your garden. After the gardening season, allow your chickens into your garden, and they will do the work for you. They will gobble up any insects and pests that are in the soil and uproot the unwanted weeds. They will dig through the topsoil and consume any damaged vegetables that might be lingering in the soil. They will pick through the remnants of any leftover vegetables such as carrot tops, broccoli stems, chard, and kale. After they are done, they will scratch through the topsoil and mix it up in the process.

Chickens are not only a source of meat and eggs, but they also produce good quality manure in the form of chicken litter, and you can collect up to one cubic foot of manure from a single fowl. Chicken litter serves as good natural fertilizer, and it can be easily composted, aged, and added to your vegetable or herb garden.

While cleaning the chicken coop, you can collect and pile up the chicken litter and any organic bedding material that you use. The best manure is obtained by maintaining a ratio of two parts of chicken litter to one part of bedding materials. To make the compost more nutrient-rich, you can also add in scraps of vegetables, fruits, twigs, leaves, and shredded paper. Add a small quantity of water to facilitate the decomposition of your compost mix. Soaking the pile of compost and stirring it regularly to add air will give you a good mix of manure, to eradicate any unwanted bacteria, maintain a temperature between 130 degrees Fahrenheit and 150 degrees Fahrenheit.

Bees

If you have a small backyard or a garden, you can raise bees and become a beekeeper. Raising bees takes about the same amount of effort and time that it takes to grow vegetables or herbs in your vegetable garden. The best part about beekeeping is that the bees help your vegetables, flowers, and any other garden plants to grow and proliferate. Their active involvement in the pollination of plants makes them a very valuable asset in gardening.

The endgame, however, is the delicious honey that they produce. Honey is one of the rare food products that never perishes or goes bad. With the ongoing bee crisis and the drastic decline in their population, beekeeping will also give you a sense of satisfaction, when you help this critical pollinator in a time of crisis. There are a number of things that you need to look into before becoming a backyard beekeeper, but don't be overwhelmed; taking care of bees is no different than taking care of any other animal, such as chickens or llamas.

As a beginner, a backyard is a good place to start, but since there is the question of safety, don't take the bees, zoning, neighbors, and your family for granted. Make sure to check if the zoning authority in your local area permits beekeeping. You don't want to violate any laws or zoning rules because you may end up breaking them if you aren't aware of what you are doing.

Getting a Hive Stand

Your hives should be off the ground to prevent any unwanted insects and other critters from entering the hive and contaminating it. You can either purchase a ready-made hive stand, or you can even construct it yourself. A hive stand is typically easy to construct and is pretty inexpensive. The hive should be around eighteen inches above the ground to prevent skunks, ants and other unwanted critters from entering the hive. Each hive is equally spaced to provide room for placing the covers and honey supers. This lets you examine the hives later on in the season. Setting the hive components without providing any space between the hive stands and the ground is also hard on your back, and lifting them becomes a much harder thing than it needs to be.

Protecting Yourself

One important thing to keep in mind regarding beekeeping is protection. You will need protective gear of some sort if you do not want to be stung by your bees. You can use a veil or a protective helmet, which keeps errant bees from getting entangled in your hair or stinging your face.

A simple hat and veil combo are what most beekeepers prefer to use, especially when it's hot and sunny outside, and there is not much dirty work involved. If you are concerned about getting stung on your body, you can use a lightweight jacket with a veil attached to it. You want to keep yourself clean and protected while doing regular bee work, but you don't necessarily require a full suit to keep yourself safe. Most beekeeping veils can be unzipped, and you can throw it back if you need to have a drink or answer your phone.

If you are doing heavy-duty bee work, a full bee suit and gloves are essential. If the weather isn't perfect, it can irritate the bees, and they might be more aggressive than you're accustomed to. If you are working in the dark, you will need to work fast. Having a bee suit and gloves will help you work quickly and efficiently without having to worry about getting stung. If you are a beginner and this is your first attempt at raising bees, the first few times you have bees walking over your fingers and hands might be distracting, so a bee suit will help you ease into the process. If you find that wearing the bee suit feels uncomfortable or restricts your movement, a veil and gloves are a good place to start.

Get a Smoker

A "smoker" is a beekeeper's most important tool. It is a cylinder with a bellow attached to it. A slow-burning fire is built inside the cylinder. You can use pine needles, old burlap, dry wood, or commercially produced smoker fuel. The smoke produced by this slow-burning flame is blown out by contracting the bellows. The smoke comes out of the narrow nozzle of the smoker and enters the beehive, causing the bees to leave the hives and seek safety. While the bees are busy, you can harvest the honey.

There are many environmental benefits of beekeeping, and it is also a source of food. The act of raising bees not only gives you the reward of harvesting honey, but it also has a very positive impact on the growth of vegetables and fruits, especially if you have a garden. Honey is one of the most fascinating substances that we know of; it is made from the nectars of different flowers, and it never goes rank or stale.

Not only is it tasty, but it is also very beneficial for the body. It has anti-microbial and anti-bacterial properties, which make it a great remedy for allergies. It can also be applied to burns and wounds. Honey is used in a variety of skin care products such as bath oils, shampoos, and creams. Bees also produce other useful substances such as royal jelly, propolis, and beeswax. Propolis or bee glue is made from the sticky resins that are found in trees. The substance can be found in between the entrances of the hives. Royal jelly is the food supply of the hive's queen. It has powerful anti-bacterial properties, and it is also considered to be a super-food, as it contains enzymes, fatty acids, amino acids, vitamins, chelated minerals, and polyphenols.

The sheer variety of output that a hive of bees can dish out makes it the best choice of livestock to raise at home. Considering the ongoing bee population crisis and the drastic decline in their population, and their importance in the ecosystem, trying to increase their numbers by providing a safe haven will help the environment in the long run.

Livestock

To raise cattle at home, you have a limited number of choices if you have limited space. Goats are a convenient way of raising livestock with limited space, but their need for grazing requires an adequate amount of grass, and some good fencing. Before buying a goat, think about what you are raising them for, dairy or meat.

Apart from the nutritious goat milk, you can also make cheese, butter, and other dairy products out of the fat-rich milk. The average lifespan of a goat ranges between fifteen years to eighteen years, and with the danger of predation removed, a goat can maintain a high output of dairy for a long period of time.

Goats do not require a lot of work in terms of taking care of them; all you need to do is keep them dry, disease and tick free, and well-fed. A small three-sided cage with a roof is enough for standard climates. You can use padded dirt or hay to create the floor of the goat house and keep them warm and dry. Since hay is also a part of a goat's diet, you will have to replace it periodically. The important thing to remember is fencing; goats require a very sturdy enclosure so that they don't climb over it.

Pigs are a good source of meat, and although their docile nature makes them very easy to raise, you are not allowed to raise them in cities or urban areas. If you are living in a rural place, you can raise a few pigs on a small piece of land. You need a pen where they can take shelter; you can use hay for insulating the floor and make a dry bedding arrangement. Pigs require a lot of food in the form of proteins and vegetables. The problem that arises when you raise pigs for meat is butchering them. Since most people don't have access to the equipment, the only option is to take it to a slaughterhouse and harvest the meat.

Chapter Seven: Dealing with Plant Pests and Diseases

Imagine yourself heading out on an early summer morning and walking into your organic garden, expecting to find the strong and healthy plants that you were tending to on the previous day, only to find the apparent signs of a plant infestation. The plants that you tended to with so much care and love seemingly withered overnight, and it looks like something is eating away at them. That could easily be any gardener or horticulturist's worst nightmare. As an organic farmer/gardener who relies on themselves for vegetables and fruits, it can be one of the most devastating experiences. You may have thought about using pesticides, but how would that affect your family's health? What about the soil or the groundwater? How will these chemicals affect them, and the more important question is, do you want to find out the answer to that question? No gardener likes watching pests or diseases wreak havoc on a garden that is teaming with healthy and organic produce. Fortunately, there are a number of ways of keeping these unwelcome visitors away from your plants. You can prevent and control different garden pests and diseases through natural and artificial measures. There may be some type of pesticides that are strong and detrimental to the beneficial bugs and critters that help your plants by keeping the soil fertile, make sure you control their use. We'll now take a look at some of the common garden pests and different ways of dealing with them naturally.

Aphids

Aphids are tiny, pear-shaped insects with soft bodies; they are green, gray, pink, yellow, and black in color. Aphids have long antennae and two small-feeder tubes that project rearward from their abdomen. Some aphids can also have transparent wings that fold over their backs, allowing them to fly. They can be found in most vegetables, fruits, and flowers throughout the world. Aphids reproduce fast, and they can take over plants very quickly. Since they usually congregate and nest on the underside of flowers and leaves of fruits and vegetables, they can be very hard to spot until they become too big of a menace and pose a real problem. Produce that is infested by aphids can easily be spotted by curled leaves, sticky stems, and yellowish spots.

Some easy methods of controlling aphids are:

● Wash your produce with a strong spray of water. A good wash can remove any residual eggs or small bugs that may be lingering on the vegetables or fruits that you harvest.

● Allow native predators such as ladybugs and lacewings to proliferate in your garden. Ladybugs can defend your plants against aphids. If you set a ladybug nettle (a group of ladybug eggs) in your garden, the resulting ladybug population can eat up to 5000 aphids every year, and they will continue to reproduce and protect your garden for a long time.

● If feasible, construct a floating row cover for your organic garden. These semi-permeable enclosures allow sunlight and air to interact with the plants, but the aphids and other small pests are kept outside.

Home Remedies

Here are some natural remedies that have proven to be effective in controlling aphid populations in a garden.

- Spray some garlic juice or water infused with hot pepper onto your plants to avoid aphids from infesting it. For severe infestations, horticultural oil, neem oil or insecticidal soap can be sprayed as a repellent. Just make sure that you wash the produce after harvesting it.

- Add one tablespoon of grated orange or lemon rind to a pint of boiling water. Allow the solution to rest overnight and strain it using a sieve or filter. Pour the filtered solution into an atomizer and spray it onto the surface of the leaves. Make sure that the leaves are saturated with the solution on both sides. Reapply the solution after every seven days or as needed to avoid the onset of aphids.

- Take a cup of water and add a teaspoon of dishwashing liquid and a teaspoon of vegetable oil. Spray your plants with this solution, making sure that both sides of the leaves are soaked with the solution. After two or three hours, rinse off your plants with a gardening can or hose. Repeat the process after every few days.

Beetles

Several species of beetles eat plant matter and can infest your organic garden. Beetles can be found on leaves of vegetables, potatoes, tomatoes, eggplants, peppers, and flowers. These critters defoliate the plants, killing off the younger plants and reducing the yield of the ones that survive. Some of the common types of beetles, which can infest and decimate plants are flea beetles, vine weevils, Colorado potato beetles, asparagus beetles, Mexican bean beetles, and Japanese beetles. The good thing about a beetle infestation is that it is much easier for you to spot, unlike whiteflies and aphids.

Some easy remedies for controlling beetles are:

- Construct floating row covers for your garden. These semi-permeable sheets keep the beetles at bay while allowing the plant to receive sunlight and oxygen.

- Using mulch, such as deep straw mulch, can help prevent bugs and other garden critters from infesting your precious vegetables and fruits. Not only does it serve as a form of pest control, but it also helps to retain moisture and cut out weeds and unwanted seedlings.

- Many bugs are easy to spot, and you can remove them by hand. Just make sure that you have your gardening gloves on so that you don't get stung. Some bugs can give you nasty skin rashes, so make sure that your skin is protected.

- Attractive native predator species such as ladybugs and lacewings can also help to reduce the population of beetles.

Home Remedies

- A natural way of getting rid of beetles from your plants is by using a bucket of soapy water. You can pour the solution on the plants and rinse them after half an hour. Pouring soapy water over infested plants can help control the infestation. Taking a hands-on approach, you can handpick the beetles from the leaves and stems and drop them into the bucket of water.

- If soapy water does not work and you continue to see beetles after applying the soap solution, you can try spraying neem oil solution on your plants instead. Neem-oil based sprays and solutions are obtained from the seeds of fruits of the neem plant. Since it is an organic pesticide, it only targets the critters without killing any useful organism and contaminating the soil or water supply.

Snails

Snails and slugs are found in damp and dark conditions. Snails can be one of the most destructive pests that a gardener dreads finding in their garden. Although they may move slowly, they work continuously throughout the night to climb up the plants and eat any tender buds or leaves. If your garden is infested by snails, you will come across shiny, slimy trails on stones and other hard surfaces.

Home Remedies

- You can make your garden less appealing to snails and slugs by being more vigilant and removing any unnecessary weeds and undergrowth. Watering your plants during the morning instead of watering them at night can reduce the chances of snail infestations.

- The simplest way of getting rid of snails and slugs is by placing a few wooden boards in your vegetable garden. Snails and slugs take refuge under the wooden boards during the night. In the morning, remove the wooden boards and scrape off the snails and slugs into a trashcan. Make sure that you securely tie the bag and dispose of it afterward.

- A crafty method of getting rid of snails and slugs is to trap them using homemade traps made of glass jars containing a few scoops of cornmeal. Place the open jar sideways in your garden during the night. In the morning, you will find snails and dead slugs that are stuck inside the jar. Repeat the process until you get rid of all the pests.

- A similar way of getting rid of snails and slugs is using beer. Fill empty cans or bowls up to the brim with beer and leave them in your garden overnight. Snails and slugs are attracted to the beer, and they will crawl and fall into the containers, drowning and dying. You can throw out the dead critters in the morning and repeat the process whenever you want to.

- If you are growing your plants in flowerpots, a simple way of avoiding snail and slug infestations is to rub Vaseline on the rim and surface of the flowerpot. Snails cannot climb up the flowerpots because of the slippery surface, and your plants will remain unharmed.

Mites

Mites or spider mites can damage leafy greens, forming lightly speckled spots. The leaves of mite-infested plants are curled and develop a yellow shade. You might also find some small webs on your plants. To identify a spider mite infestation, take a leaf and hold it over a piece of white paper and tap it. You can see tiny mites on the paper using a magnifying glass.

Home Remedies

• Add three tablespoons of liquid dishwashing soap into one gallon of water and mix them well. Use the solution to soak the plants thoroughly and leave it for a few hours. Rinse the plants with your garden hose afterward. Repeat the process after every week to keep spider mites away.

• Another easy DIY organic method of controlling mite infestations is with alcohol solution. Mix two parts of water with one part of alcohol and mist the solution on mite-infested plants. You should do this at night so that the alcohol has evaporated before the morning.

Earwigs

Earwigs are also known as pincher bugs. They feed on decomposing plant matter and wet or rotting leaves. They can infest your garden and can even find their way into the house during the summer and monsoon seasons.

Home Remedies

• The easiest way of getting rid of earwigs is by placing rolls of wet newspaper in and around your vegetable garden during the evening. Earwigs are nocturnal creatures and are more active during the night. They will crawl into the damp paper, and you can get rid of them the next morning. Carefully dispose of the rolled newspaper into a garbage bag and get rid of them as soon as you can.

Ants

Ants are more prevalent in hotter regions, and they can appear in the hundreds overnight indoors and outdoors. A safe remedy for avoiding ants from infesting your kitchen cabinets is sprinkling powdered cinnamon, red chili pepper, dried peppermint, or paprika. Sprinkle them along the paths where you normally find ants.

Home Remedies

• If you come across an ant colony in your garden, you can pour boiling water into the entrance of the colony during the morning. All ants do not remain inside the nest all day long, and you might not get rid of all of them if you do this during the day.

• Spray small quantities of white vinegar around the stems of the plants that are infested by ants.

• Sprinkle a pinch of cornmeal or plain sugar near the entrances of the ant colony, ants are attracted to sugar and cornmeal, and not only do they eat it, but they also bring it back inside the colony for the other ants to eat. Lacing the sugar with an insecticide can do the trick. Cornmeal naturally expands inside their stomach after they ingest it, so poisoning it is not necessary.

Grasshoppers

Grasshoppers are found in specific seasons of the year, specifically the months of spring and the monsoon season. They devour growing leaves and flowers and can do a lot of damage to your organic garden. Since these insects are larger than most pests, controlling grasshopper infestations can be very tricky.

Home Remedies

• The best option is spraying your plants with a garlic solution. You can crush two bulbs of garlic and blend them in ten cups of water. Heat the solution and let it sit for a day. Remove the residue using a sieve. Mix the solution with three parts of water and fill it in a spray bottle. Spray the garlic-water solution on both sides of the leaves and the stems to repel grasshoppers from devouring your tasty produce.

• Growing vegetables such as sweet clover, calendula, and cilantro can help control the grasshopper population. The smell of these plants acts as a repellent against grasshoppers.

Tomato Hornworms

As the name suggests, hornworms are three or four-inch worms that feast on tomatoes. They can also be found in gardens that have eggplants, peppers, and potatoes. They are green in color, and can be easy to miss in the vegetation, but they can cause a lot of damage to your garden.

Home Remedies

• These worms are resistant to most organic pesticides, so the best way of getting rid of them is by picking them off by hand and drowning them in a bucket of soapy water. Using stronger chemicals and insecticides may help you to get rid of the hornworms, but they also kill organisms that are beneficial for your garden.

• If you notice any hornworms carrying white spots, you can leave them alone. The white spots are wasp egg sacks, and they will eventually hatch and attack the host, solving your pest problem for you.

Scale Bugs

Scale bugs are pests commonly found in warm and dry climates; they are very small in size and appear as tiny orange-colored or rust-colored bumps. Some species of scale bugs are also capable of secreting sticky honeydew, which makes your plants more vulnerable to fungal infections and diseases. A scale bug infestation causes the leaves of a plant to turn yellow, wither, and fall off. If left undeterred, they can kill the entire plant.

Home Remedies

• Scale bugs are incapable of flying, so if you find a few of them on a leaf of lettuce, you can simply get rid of the affected portion and use the rest.

• If you did not catch the infestation early enough and the bugs have taken a firm hold of your plants, you can use neem oil sprays. Cut off the parts of the plants that have turned yellow. If scale bug infestations are a frequent occurrence, you can use hot pepper wax sprays to keep them from returning.

- You can make your pepper spray at home. Chop up five or six hot peppers and mix them with one tablespoon of cayenne paper along with half a gallon of water. Heat the mixture and bring it to boil for fifteen minutes. Let the mixture cool and set overnight. Strain it using a muslin cloth or coffee filter, and to the solution, add one tablespoon of dishwashing soap. Spray the solution on the bug-infested plants every five days, and you will see their numbers decreasing.

- Take four onions, two tablespoons of cayenne pepper, two cloves of garlic, and one quart of water and make a mixture using a blender. Take the mixture and add it to two gallons of water along with two tablespoons of detergent. Shake the mixture well and spray it on your plants.

- For larger bugs, you can make a mixture using crushed garlic, a cup of canola oil, a few tablespoons of hot pepper powder, and a gallon of water. Spray the solution on your plants to get rid of the larger garden critters.

Rodents and Moles

Rats, moles, voles, gerbils, ground squirrels, and other rodents are notorious pests. They can tear up a whole garden in a few minutes. Poisoning these creatures may prove to be troublesome and ethically questionable.

Home Remedies

- Digging holes or "moats" around your garden is a good way of keeping rodents away from your garden. You can also set humane mousetraps near the entrance of their burrows. Most of the time, you can find them somewhere close to your garden. Remember to use more than one trap because these rodents usually live in small groups. You can relocate these rodents after you have trapped them by letting them out near forests. This is a more humane way of getting rid of them, instead of poisoning them using pesticides and insecticides.

- If the degree of rodent infestation in your organic farm is too severe, causing damage to a lot of plants, you can consider getting dogs. Special breeds of dogs such as bloodhounds, basset hounds, Jack Russell terriers, dachshunds, and mastiffs are bred for hunting. The smaller breeds are efficient hunters, and they can be very effective in controlling large rodent infestations. Make sure that you use protective gear while hunting for rodents; running into a rabid groundhog and getting bitten by it will only lead to a lot of anti-rabies injections and personal discomfort.

- An easy way of repelling groundhogs and rats is sprinkling Epsom salts on your plants. These salts affect the taste of the plant and make them foul and unappealing to groundhogs. Sprinkling Epsom salts also enriches the soil and helps plants to grow better. If you can't get your hands on Epsom salts, you can use ammonia-soaked rags. Place them along the perimeter of your garden to create a smelly barrier. Although this may keep the rodents away, rain and dew wash away the smell, so you might have to replenish it after every week.

- Using row covers and erecting fences are the only permanent solution against rodents and other non-insect pests. Using chicken-wire fencing can be a good way of keeping out rats and moles from your garden. Some rodents such as squirrels and groundhogs can climb over fences and under tunnels. Make sure that your fences are at least three to four feet high to keep these pesky rodents out of your garden.

Chapter Eight: How to Extend the Growing Season

There are a lot of factors that affect the growth and development of plants, and climate is one of the important ones. Some places have perfect conditions for plants to grow and develop, while others have a very short growing season. Cold places such as northern Russia and Norway have long winters, and only a handful of plants are ready to grow and turn ripe before permafrost sets in. Choosing the plants that you want to grow, and choosing the right time to grow them, can make a lot of difference. There is plenty of time in between February and December for you to grow what you want to.

A good way of ensuring that you get the most out of your plants, is by extending your growing season. Don't be mistaken; the soil needs to take some time off and replenish its nutrients after a harvest, while also giving you a short break to put away the gardening tools. Sometimes it can prove to be more beneficial if you harvest your crops early. However, if you are blessed with somewhat normal climatic conditions, you can get more out of your organic garden by extending your garden season. Here are some easy ways to extend your growing season:

Reduce Wind Exposure

Strong winds can be a huge problem if you are growing plants in your garden or if you have your own homestead. If the plants in your organic garden have to battle harsh weather conditions and strong winds constantly, they will spend most of their energy on surviving these harsh conditions, instead of developing healthy root systems and producing tasty produce.

Protect your plants from strong winds by erecting wooden fences or row covers. Making a natural windbreak by planting trees and shrubs can also help to shield your plants from the harsh winds. If you have no other options left, purchase some windbreak netting from Amazon and put it up around your garden. Your main objective is reducing wind speed without completely cutting off the flow of air and creating dead calm.

If you live in a place where there are prevailing winds, you can build a fence on that side of the garden, and that in itself can be enough to keep your plants from getting battered by strong winds. Erecting a permanent fence or building a wooden one can take a lot of time and financial resources. Using temporary plastic mesh fences and row covers made of polypropylene garden fabric can be an alternative solution. Seedlings that are allowed to grow under shelter or covers can show twice as much growth as plants that are grown unprotected.

Warming up the Soil

Using mulch beds is a good way of keeping the soil warm and preventing the onset of permafrost. If you have used mulch in your garden over the winter, make sure to remove it during early spring so that the soil gets sufficient exposure to sunlight and air. You can raise the temperature of your garden soil by raising the garden beds. Another convenient way of raising the temperature of the soil is by covering the cold spring soil with a black tarpaulin or plastic covers. You can leave the plastic bags most of the time, and you only need to remove them prior to planting your saplings. Covering the soil with black plastic covers or mulch can allow heat-loving plants such as melons and berries to grow at a rapid pace. Covering the soil also helps to keep the temperature of the soil consistently warm during fall or winter. This can extend the growing season and help crops such as tomatoes, peppers, and okra to fully ripen by giving the plants a few extra weeks to grow.

Frost Protection Using Cold Covers

For many organic gardening enthusiasts, frost can be a limiting factor during early spring and winter. In colder places, the temperature can drop down to thirty-two degrees Fahrenheit during autumn and early spring, which is enough to kill all your plants in one night. Covering the soil and plants with plant covers, sheets, cardboard boxes, and blankets are good temporary solutions.

If you are looking for a more permanent way of dealing with frost, you should consider purchasing garden fabric or row covers. You must be familiar with the climate conditions of the place where you live, so be prepared to protect your plants when you think frost might set in. You can start by stocking up on cardboard boxes and grocery bags. If you are a proponent of recycling, you can use one-gallon milk jars or used tetra pack cartons. Cutting off the bottoms of the cartons or jugs makes a cheap and effective cover.

Since most containers come with caps at the top, you can unscrew them and open them during the day to release excess heat. If you have individual seedlings or saplings that are growing in your garden, you can use upside-down paper bags and anchor them in one place using small pebbles or rocks.

Row covers are available in different varieties and thicknesses for different temperatures. Cold covers and portable greenhouse enclosures can offer very good protection against frost and cold temperatures. If used properly, you can extend the harvest season of crops right through the winter, which lets you get more output out of your organic garden. You can even build your own cold covers and cold frames if you have the tools at your disposal. Cold frames are nothing more than shallow rectangular boxes without a bottom and cover on top that is usually made of transparent plastic, glass, or fiberglass. The sidewalls can be made using wood or bales of straw; the only thing you need to remember is that the sides should slope in order to capture sunlight. You can fill up the cold frame with soil or garden loam.

Most vegetables and plants become dormant at very low temperatures, so make sure to get your cold frames up during the summer so that cool-season veggies can be grown and ready for harvest during the winter or early spring. Once summer comes, you can convert these cold frames into hotbeds and grow fruits and summer veggies during the warmer months.

Successive Planting

Successive planting is the best way to extend the growing season over a period of time. One common successive planting method is to transplant seedlings and sow seeds of the same variety simultaneously. The transplants develop and ripen before the direct-seeded plants, allowing you to have two different harvests in the same growing season.

Another effective method of successive planting is to replant seeds or transplants at periodic intervals. For instance, plant radishes and spinach in one week; sow scallions, beans, salad greens, and beets once in every two weeks; and sow larger plants such as squash and vegetables after every month. Since it is impossible to predict weather patterns correctly, keep planting the seeds until they stop sprouting.

The third method of successive planting is to sow seeds of different varieties that mature at different rates. For instance, if you plant corn and peas at the same time, your harvest season will extend because of the plants maturing at different time periods. Plant carrots, salad greens, and radishes in the same row of your garden to keep a constant supply of organic produce growing at any particular time in your garden. You can mix two different varieties of seeds of lettuce and radishes and plant the mix every two weeks. If you have sufficient space in your garden, you can get organic produce of different varieties to last you for weeks. Over time, you will figure out which plants grow well in which seasons, and you can choose the ones that grow the fastest, further increasing the garden's output while also extending the growing season.

Interplanting

Interplanting is the practice of growing compatible vegetables in a single row of the garden. There are many benefits to interplanting. It helps you to extend the growing season by planting fast-growing plants along with the slow growers. By the time the slow-growing plants develop and mature, the fast-growers have already ripened and been harvested, allowing the slow-growing plants to develop and grow fully.

Another way that interplanting extends the growing season is by letting you grow vegetables that normally require cool temperatures in the hotter months of spring and summer. The shade that is created by the leaves of larger veggies such as cabbages, corn, and other tall crops significantly improves the growing conditions for cool weather crops such as lettuce and radishes.

Interplanting, similar to successive planting, keeps weeds and other unwanted vegetation from finding a foothold in your garden, and this subsequently increases your crop yield. Varying the environment and the chemistry of the soil by planting different crops discourages common pests from adapting to your garden's conditions. As an incentive, if one crop fails or does not do particularly well in a season, the interplanted crop still allows you to harvest something from your garden.

Crop Rotation

Crop rotation is the practice of planting two different vegetables or fruits of different varieties/families in different patches of soil in your garden without any repetition. Since all the plants belonging to a particular family experience the same problems while growing, crops that are grown in the rotation will have a lesser tendency of suffering from pest infestations, disease, and soil deficiencies. This method of growing crops can, therefore, produce a larger output over a long period, owing to less depletion of the soil's nutrients. Using mulch beds and trellises comes in handy during crop rotation because all that's left to do is shift the same rotational planting scheme from one bed to another. Growing legumes after every successive crop rotation is a good way of putting nitrogen back into the soil. When you grow the same type of plant in the same patch of soil in your garden, the soil is likely to be tired and devoid of all its nutrients. Crop rotation not only extends the growing season but also increases your garden's lifespan.

Water When Necessary

Over-watering your garden can cause a lot of problems. You should only water your garden to the level that it is enough to make up for the difference between the level of rainfall and the amount of water that your plants require. If your garden is fertile and enriched with organic matter, the soil is inherently capable of holding and trapping most of the moisture that falls on it, eliminating the need for you to water it. Mulching is another way of ensuring that the soil retains moisture, allowing root systems to grow and develop. The increase in moisture allows your plants to grow even through spells of moderately dry weather.

A lot of new gardeners and organic gardening enthusiasts tend to overwater their gardens. Excessive water can discourage the roots from venturing deeper into the ground and makes them stick just below the topsoil instead. As a result, the plants do not have access to all the nutrients and minerals that it needs. The overwatered roots tend to adapt to the moist conditions and dry out quickly when there is no water supply.

The water content of the soil also depends upon the rainfall that your garden receives. Too much rain can cause vegetables such as carrots, potatoes, and onions to rot in the ground, and can make cabbages and tomatoes split. For places that receive dense rainfall, you can use raised beds or trellises to deal with waterlogging and protect crops that tend to be sensitive to excess water.

You can easily tell if your garden needs water by picking up a handful of soil and squeezing it. If the lump of dirt does not hold itself together when you open your fist, it means that you need to grab the garden hose and water your garden.

Plant Early

It is easier to start the season early rather than extending it toward the end. Be ready to plant vegetables or fruits during early spring, as soon as soil dampness and soil temperature begin normalizing. It is better to use raised beds or trellises because they hold soil over the normal ground level and let it dry faster compared to normal soil in the ground. This means that you can plant your seedlings several weeks earlier than normal soil conditions would otherwise allow. If you are not familiar with using raised garden beds, try sectioning off a part of your garden and set up the raised beds as soon as you can. You can also take the extra initiative by adding soil thermometers to monitor the temperature of the soil.

A good way of getting a jumpstart is by starting seeds indoors. Seeds that are started indoors and transplanted outside tend to take off when they are shifted outdoors. You can set up your seeds three months before the season actually starts so that the saplings are ready by the time spring kicks in. When the seedlings grow up to 3 or 4 inches, you can transfer them to larger flowering pots and then move them to your garden after they cross 6 or 7 inches. By the time spring kicks in and the soils warm up enough for plants to begin growing, you will have sturdy saplings with well-developed roots resulting in more produce.

Stretching the Harvest Season

Extending your garden season depends entirely on how much time you are willing to invest in your garden. It also depends upon the climatic conditions of the place where you live. If you live in a cold country such as Norway, extending your harvest season through the most part of the year means that you will have to invest in greenhouses and provide daily attention to your garden. On the other hand, if your needs are more subtle such as extending the growing season for your heirloom tomatoes by a few weeks in the fall or transplanting your saplings in early spring, there are several easy and inexpensive solutions.

The 30-Day Stretch

Providing a safe growing environment for your plants or seedlings and keeping them protected from the sun, harsh winds, frost, and pests will give them a much faster start. When you are transplanting seedlings during the beginning of the growing season, leave them covered with garden fabric or muslin cloth for the first two weeks. You can purchase garden fabrics from organic gardens or online stores. These fabrics are made of polypropylene or spun polyester, and they allow the flow of sunlight, air, and water. This means that the excess heat can escape during hot summer days; rainwater can also enter the cover and pass-through, so you won't have to worry about waterlogged plants. Checking on your plants every day and removing weeds regularly is all that you need to do.

Since you are only extending your garden season by a thirty-day stretch, you can stick to the more temporary alternatives such as plastic milk containers, coffee cans, and cardboard boxes. Just make sure that you leave vents in the covers so that the plants do not get overheated.

The 60-Day Stretch

For extending the growing season by one or two months, you will have to make use of garden fabrics. During the warmer months of spring and summer, you can use the temporary solutions that are mentioned above but switch them for a heavier garden fabric during the fall or winter. Heavier soil covers are functional at lower temperatures, and they help the soil to retain heat and prevent the onset of frost and damage.

Choosing the right plant varieties for the right seasons can make a very significant difference. Some varieties of plants are more suited to grow during early spring, whereas some of them grow well into late autumn. For instance, there are some varieties of broccoli that thrive in a cold spring, and there are varieties of broccoli that are capable of tolerating heat. Some plants may thrive with the help of sunlight, whereas some plants grow well in low-light conditions.

3- or 4-Month Stretch

Extending your garden season by three or four months means that you can extend your harvest season all year round. In many parts of the world that experience cold weather and have short growing seasons, there is no option but to use tents or greenhouses. Maintaining a consistent and protected growing environment in the face of harsh and fluctuating weather conditions is actually easier than it sounds. The rewards of having healthy and organic produce throughout the year outweighs the initial investments that you make.

The key to successfully extending your growing season by three or four months is to focus on a small number of crops or a particular section of your garden. Trying to extend the growing season for a large area requires a lot of investment and raw materials. You are better off sectioning your garden and using smaller three ft x four ft sections to grow different vegetables. If you choose the right variety of plants to grow, a small section like this can provide you with many months' worth of food. Use cold covers or cold frames and garden fabric to make small enclosures and grow vegetables or fruits throughout eight to ten months of the year.

Chapter Nine: Preparing Your Kitchen for the Harvest

The harvest season is right around the corner if you notice the leaves changing their colors and getting ready for the winter. When autumn comes along, it brings with it the season of harvest. Besides Halloween, and pumpkin spice lattes, October is also the time for harvesting seeds and reaping the fruits of your labor. Every organic gardening enthusiast dreams of a huge organic garden with plants that produce healthy and organic food. However, if you are not used to having a flourishing organic garden yielding lots of food, you may become overwhelmed when it becomes a reality for you.

Whether you are growing salad greens and tomatoes or fruits such as strawberries and raspberries, you will want every bit of your homegrown produce to be useful. Seeing things go to waste during the harvest season can be a bitterly discouraging experience. There is only so much salad and apple pie that you and your family can eat, so preserving some fruits and vegetables or making jams and pickles is a good way of utilizing all the produce. Doing this can also save you a lot of money and time that is normally spent buying groceries and vegetables, and it also provides ample food during the winters. In case you are getting ready for your first harvest season, this chapter will provide you with all the information that you need to make the most of your fresh organic produce.

The harvest season can take a newcomer by surprise. Although very rare, it might even make an experienced organic gardener emotional. No, you will not be emotional or tearful when you bring in your first homegrown cucumber into the kitchen. What I'm talking about is the exhaustion and fatigue that comes after a long day of canning pickles or shucking cherries. Although it is a thrill for most people to harvest a rich and healthy bounty from their gardens, some can find it overwhelming and tiring to repeatedly harvest and process large amounts of fruits and vegetables. Harvesting crops from your organic garden might need more energy and work than you anticipate, so make sure that you are mentally ready before beginning the process.

When you are finding ways of preparing yourself for the harvest season, there are two things that you need to aspire to:

Keeping Your Kitchen Clean and Efficient

Having a clean and clutter-free kitchen can increase your kitchen's functionality and capacity to store food. You can declutter the kitchen by making use of organizers and labeling things that need labeling. Using organizers, clear containers, spice racks, and cabinet bins can save you a lot of space and time that is usually spent digging through piles of packages and finding a sachet of paprika. Having drawer organizers that help to segregate dishes, spoons, and other types of cutlery, keeps your kitchen and pantry tidy. If you are looking for permanent ways to make your kitchen more efficient, you can consider investing in kitchen appliances that perform multiple functions and make your life easier.

Keeping Your Food Fresh

Planting an organic garden and harvesting the fruits takes a lot of hard work and time. After your fruits and vegetables have ripened, and they become ready for harvesting, you might want to check on your refrigerator to make sure that it is working. You want to keep your food as crisp as possible, for as long as possible. Preserving food is always an option, but you would prefer anything that's fresh over the same thing in pickled form. Having a good understanding of different storage techniques and knowing which fruits and veggies belong in low humidity or high humidity conditions can provide a lot of help. Avoid storing perishable items such as bananas, tomatoes, and onions inside the fridge.

The harvest season can be hectic while you are trying to collect and store everything that your organic garden provided you with. An average backyard garden can produce up to seventy-five pounds of food within a week. That is not exactly a small quantity, and trying to keep up with everything at the very last moment can be problematic. Here are some things that may help you to deal with the challenges of the harvest season:

Finish Other Projects

The biggest mistake that organic gardening enthusiasts make before their first harvest season is to have other major projects or commitments at the same time. Not setting aside sufficient time during the harvest season distracts you from taking care of the healthy bounties that your garden provides for you after the long growing season. The same goes for anyone who is responsible for helping you with other activities such as food preservation and storage. The harvest season can be a great opportunity for you and your family to be collectively involved in something, so make sure that everyone involved in the harvesting activities remains available during the harvest season.

Make Sure You Have Help

This goes hand in hand with the previous step; make sure that you have people to help you through the harvesting process. Another common mistake that most beginners make is thinking that you can do everything on your own. Harvesting can be a lengthy and cumbersome process, and the amount of work that goes into it might be too much for a single person to handle. You can involve your kids in the process, especially if they are on the younger side and need constant supervision. The collective activity can be good for the child's social development, while also letting you take care of your kids and get work done simultaneously.

Make a Plan

As the famous saying goes, failing to plan is planning to fail. The idea of having your own organic garden that yields lots of produce is a good one, but have you thought about what you are going to do once the produce is harvested? There is a limit to the amount of food that you can preserve and store, so what will you do? Will you be ready for the harvest season, and will you have sufficient resources to store all the food?

There are a lot of ways to streamline this process; you can play around with the types of plants that you choose to grow in your garden, and you can also harvest different crops in different seasons to make things easier for you. Planning what ingredients you need and acquiring them beforehand can save you from a mountain of work piling up at the very last moment.

Check Your Preservatives

If this is the first time that you are dealing with a large harvest, you might not be too familiar with the different preservation processes. Before the harvest season kicks in, make sure that you have read up on what's necessary and figured out which preservation methods to use. Depending on how much produce you harvest, there is a good chance that you will require plenty of spices, vinegar, sugar, sweeteners, lemons and other natural preservatives. You can save money by purchasing these commodities in bulk from a wholesaler or supplier and acquire what you need at a discount instead of purchasing them from normal retail stores. Other useful accessories such as cellophane paper and rubber bands can also be bought in bulk, saving you a lot of money and trouble.

Here are a few common preservation methods that you can use:

- For fruits, including tomatoes, and watery vegetables, such as cucumber and gourd, water bath canning is the best way to go.
- For fleshy vegetables and meat, pressure canning is the only way of storing them while keeping them safe for consumption at the same

time. If you are preserving lots of food, consider getting additional jars and airtight containers.

● Dehydration is one of the oldest preservation methods, and it is used for storing meat and other perishable products. You cannot dehydrate products without a dehydrator, so getting one should be at the top of the list if you plan to make dry food. In fact, a dehydrator can be so useful that having just one may not be enough for a good harvest season.

● Freezing is an effective way of storing food for a long period of time. However, if the freezer stops working or in case of a lengthy power outage, you might end up losing a lot of food. Most experts recommend dehydrating or canning the food because you do not have to rely on a freezer that is prone to fail at any given moment in time.

Using Disinfectants

The last thing you want is for your organic vegetables and fruits to get contaminated by chemicals or bacteria. You should use natural disinfectants to clean kitchen countertops and other exposed surfaces where you usually work. You will be handling a lot of food products during the harvest season, from making fruit jams to dehydrating vegetables and preserving meat. Using disinfectants and keeping your kitchen clean can avoid contamination or bacterial infections. You can make your own organic disinfectant using simple kitchen ingredients such as lemon, lime, baking soda, or apple cider vinegar.

Creating the Right Climate For Storage

Food can become rank or begin decomposing above certain temperatures. If you do not get the temperature of your storage space right, all the hard work that you put in during the growing season and harvesting can go to waste. If you have a pantry that is located in the basement, maintaining the temperature and keeping it cool is comparatively easy. However, if you have a normal kitchen without a basement, you should consider investing in a climate control system to make sure that your efforts and energy do not go to waste. Faulty storage space can undo all the hard work that goes into the process of organic farming.

Collecting Containers

If your garden is booming and it looks like harvest season is around the corner, you should start collecting glass jars or containers for keeping preserved food such as jams and pickles. You can purchase them at a local farmer's market or at yard sales and convenience stores. Always look for containers that have an airtight lid, so you don't have to worry about anything getting contaminated by air or bacteria. They're also easier to open and close, and you can even decorate them according to your taste. If you're looking, you might even find an ad in the local newspapers about people simply giving away old jam jars for free. If you are harvesting a lot of produce from your organic garden, the only way to keep it from spoiling is by preservation methods, and airtight glass jars have always been the go-to. A kitchen cabinet that is loaded with jars of preserved food is always a satisfying thing.

Invest in a Chest Freezer

If your ventures into organic gardening become successful, expect tons of produce, and be ready to store them right away. If you are growing vegetables such as pumpkins, peas, leafy greens, and beans, storing them quickly is important because they can start deteriorating quickly. A chest freezer is the best option if you don't want to bother yourself with the hassle of cooking and/or preserving them. The nutritional value of vegetables remains the same, even when you freeze them. Larger industrial-sized chest freezers provide enough space for you to store enough food to last for two to three months. Although your electricity bill might run a little high, that would be negligible compared to what you're saving by maintaining your own food supply. The good clearly outweighs the bad in this case. One thing about freezing food that you have to remember is that you do not have to spend a lot of time and energy on the preservation process, which can be pretty lengthy, especially if you have lots of produce to handle. Storage also becomes a problem if you have too many jars and containers containing everything from veggies to meat products. One large chest freezer saves you from doing a lot of work.

Modern technology has made power outages a rare thing, and even if one occasionally happens, it barely crosses the thirty-minute mark. Frozen food does not melt instantly, especially if it's been frozen for a long time; the things in your chest freezer stay fresh long enough to last during these rare power outages. Since the dawn of the 2020 pandemic, a post-apocalyptic world does not just seem like a dystopian dream, so I'd still keep a few empty jars just in case things ramp up.

Organizing Your Kitchen and Pantry

Keeping your kitchen and pantry organized is not about making drastic changes, but rather about making smaller adjustments that eventually accumulate to create a positive change. For instance, it is easier for you to tell how much food is left in a container if you use clear containers. Thus, clear containers and glass jars become a much better option; plus, paper bags or plastic bags cannot be stored in neat stacks or rows.

Tossing things into a bag and sticking them in a cupboard or drawer can become a very bad habit that is difficult to lose. Soon you find yourself losing things at the back of the cupboard or spending lots of time rummaging through piles of paper bags. Keeping your kitchen and pantry organized is the byproduct of good practices. Store food in one clear container instead of using several smaller containers; this helps you to save a lot of space and also lets you see what you have at a simple glance. Half-gallon jars and Mason glass jars are convenient for storing food, seeds, and pickles. For bulk food items, use a large container in your cooking area or pantry. For instance, you can use large glass containers to store grains or flour, then you won't have to run to the pantry every time you need them, which saves you a lot of time.

Try keeping similar items in the same containers. You can divide your rations and keep all the dry items, such as flour and grains in one cupboard and a different cupboard for wet products such as pickles, sauces, and jams. You can also use bins for storing products that are specifically used for one purpose; for instance, you can store all your baking ingredients such as flour, baking soda, yeast, and essences. Preserved food products and canned foods should be stored in cool and dry containers or cupboards. Use a single shelf for storing canned nuts, dried tomatoes, dehydrated vegetables, and other wet products.

The Purpose of Organizing Your Kitchen

An organized kitchen makes your work easy. We've all made the mistake of purchasing something that was already tucked away in our kitchen cabinets. You might have gone to the convenience store to get a can of coconut cream, only to come home and find that you already had two cans of coconut cream on the shelf. Not only do you end up wasting your own time going to the store or rummaging through your cupboard, but you also spend money unnecessarily on extra gas to drive to the store and purchasing things that you already have. It can become a vicious cycle. You might have to change recipes while you're in the thick of it, after finding out that there's not enough flour inside the containers. You can take care of all of these problems by keeping your kitchen space organized and decluttering it every once in a while.

Deciding What to Keep and What to Lose

When you decide to spend the day decluttering your kitchen, you have to make sure that you only keep what you need. Hoarding only increases inconvenience, and most people don't realize that they are doing it. If you are caught in a dilemma between keeping something and chucking it in the bin, ask yourself if you use it often. You are better off only storing things that can be used every day, weekly, or at least once in a month. If there is another item in your kitchen cupboard that is used for the same purpose: for instance, you don't need a pitcher and a punch bowl, you can do away with one of them to conserve storage space and reduce clutter.

Another good way of keeping a clutter-free kitchen is by keeping things in the correct spot. For instance, you don't need your cutlery, such as forks and spoons, to be on top of the kitchen counter. It makes better sense to stick them in a drawer instead and use the vacated space for storing things that require more use. Most kitchen drawers are filled to the brim with things that are not needed, some of them not even being used in the kitchen. You might think that it's better to empty them and start from scratch, but you might end up getting rid of things that are actually useful. For instance, if you have an old kitchen appliance that broke down and is not repairable, and cannot be recycled, throwing it in the garbage is the only thing that you can do. Recycle, give away, and sell what you can. But don't be afraid to be ruthless about throwing away things, just make sure that what you throw is actually useless. Sometimes, it's easy to be disillusioned into thinking that your kitchen or pantry is organized, even if it actually isn't. If you have piles of knick-knacks lying around in different places, it's time to get things in order.

Chapter Ten: Preserving Your Food

In this section, you will learn how to pursue the various techniques of food preservation to enhance your food supply throughout the year. We will explore canning, drying, pickling, fermenting, freezing, smoking, and cold storage of food. I have also mentioned some recipes for you to try to preserve your produce. You will also learn about the various equipment such as dehydrators and pressure cookers that will assist you.

Learning how to preserve food safely at home is a skill that you should try to master. It helps you to stock up on all the extra produce and save a lot of money. Preserving fresh produce from your farm will taste a lot better than the ones you buy commercially. These don't have any harmful preservatives or additives, either. You can sell them as organic products in farmers' markets too.

There are many different ways that you can preserve the food grown from your farm:

Minimal Processing

The easiest way to preserve food is using room temperature and cool storage. This includes using an unheated pantry and root cellaring: crawl spaces, root cellars, unheated basement space, in-ground clamps, et cetera. Vegetables such as potatoes, cabbage, carrots, beets, onions, and garlic can be stored for months. Some vegetables such as pumpkins, squash, dry corn, and root vegetables require very little processing.

Dehydrating or Drying

One of the oldest methods of food preservation is dehydrating or drying. This can be done using sun ovens, air-drying, hang drying, commercial dehydrators, and solar dehydrators, et cetera. When you have limited storage space, it is better to dry foods than to try other preservation methods. However, there are certain foods that do not dehydrate well. The dehydrated foods can be stored well in a dry and cool area for longer shelf life. Fruits, meat jerky, and vegetables dehydrate quite well for the most part.

Canning

Canning is done by heat processing food and storing it in jars for preservation. This can be done by steam canning, water bath canning, or pressure canning. In water bath canning, a large stockpot is used. Jars are placed on a canning rack without direct contact with the bottom of the stockpot. They are covered with a couple of inches of water at the bottom. High acid foods are preserved well with water bath canning. This includes tomatoes, fruits, jellies, pickles, and relishes. Steam canning has only been approved for home preservation again quite recently. A special canner is used to process food with steam without pressure. This works well for high acid foods as well. A pressure canner can be used with water bath canning if you leave the vent open. However, you have to be careful while doing this so that steam does not build up inside. Pressure canning itself is done with a pressure canner that uses high temperatures and high pressure for the preservation of foods. This method is used for preserving low acid foods such as corn, meats, carrots, beans, and sauces. It is important to follow safe canning practices, or else it can cause botulism poisoning.

Freezing

Freezing foods for preservation will require very little equipment and allows the food to retain its fresh flavor. To freeze most vegetables, you have to blanch or cook them in order to stop the action of enzymes and ensure higher quality. Blanching the foods involves treating them with heat and then immersing them quickly in cold water to stop them from being cooked. Vegetables are usually blanched for about three minutes while doing this. While freezing fruits, blanching is not usually necessary. They can be stored in their natural form or with sugars and other antioxidants that will slow down discoloration and extend storage life. You can easily freeze your fruits on cookie sheets and then place them in packets that are vacuum sealed. This allows long-term storage of frozen fruits. By sealing them in vacuum-sealed bags, you can prevent the formation of ice crystals. This also allows for the storage life to be increased nearly four times longer.

Freeze Drying

Freeze-drying or lyophilization has only been allowed in homes recently. You need a heavy-duty freezer for this, along with an airtight chamber that holds a vacuum while being used. You will also need to add a high-end vacuum pump that has extremely strong suction power. Then you need a heater and a thermostat that allows you to turn the temperature up and down. This will help you to repeat the process of sublimation for many hours. A humidity sensor is added to ensure the water remains out, and this completes the cycle of freeze-drying. Dairy products and some other foods don't store very well with other processes. This is why freeze-drying can be a beneficial preservation method to add to your homestead.

Fermentation

The fermentation of foods has been commonly practiced in many cultures over the years. Here, low acidic foods are turned into high acidic ones to increase their shelf life. They can then be stored for longer this way, or by canning them in water bath canners. There are certain starter cultures, salt or whey that can be used for fermenting foods. These ingredients help to increase the nutritious value of food and also make it easier to digest. This is why fermented food is often called live culture food. In the fermentation process, microbes will pre-digest the food, and acidity is involved. This causes changes in the texture and flavor of the food. Cheese, kombucha, yogurt, chocolate, kimchi, vinegar, sourdough bread, and sauerkraut are some foods created with fermentation.

Salt and Sugar Preservation

Salt and sugar have been used for preservation since long before other methods, such as canning or freezing, were discovered. These ingredients help to draw the liquid out of fruits, vegetables, and meat. This prevents the growth of microbes that only thrive in water. Salt and sugar will cause a change in the texture and flavor of foods. This is why you should only use them if you have the palate for it. You can preserve the herbs from your garden with salt and sugar as well.

Alcohol Immersion

Alcohol draws out water from food like salt and sugar and inhibits the growth of microbes. All you have to do is submerge a little of the produce in some hard liquor. This allows the food to be stored for a very long time. However, it is important not to put too much food in very little alcohol. Alcohol immersion is a good way to preserve foods that are highly acidic and also for making flavor extracts.

Vinegar Pickling

A highly acidic environment is not conducive to microbe growth. This is why vinegar can be used for preserving food without canning or heating. This is how pickle barrels were used to prepare long-lasting pickles.

Olive Oil Immersion

Olive oil is commonly used in Europe to preserve food. However, if you are inexperienced with it, it is best not to depend on this method. The fruit or vegetable is immersed in olive oil and locked in without air. However, if it is a low acid food, there is a high risk of botulism.

As you can see, you have many different preservation methods to use for your produce that is harvested from your farm. You can try them according to your budget, and also the specific food that you want to preserve.

You may wonder which method is best for preservation, but the answer to this question will vary. It will depend entirely on what you want to store and the storage conditions and how you go about the process. Some people say that freezing is better than canning, because the latter causes a loss of nutrients. However, studies have shown that refrigeration also causes nutrient loss after a few days. The reason behind this is that the foods continue metabolization even while they are being stored. Root cellar storage also causes nutrient loss. Dried food will also have a significant nutrient loss. This is why it is best to can food right after harvesting it, while the nutrient value is at its peak. This allows better nutrient retention for a longer period of time. Fermentation is a method that adds nutritional value to your foods, but these will only last for a few months or weeks, depending on the food. Dried foods have a longer shelf life than other preserved foods. These also occupy much less space. Freezing or drying foods allows you to store them for about two-to-three years if vacuum sealing is done. However, regardless of the method of preservation, you will find your home-preserved food much more nutritious, and safer to consume than commercially preserved food.

Some preservation recipes you can try:

Canned Apples
Supplies
- 5 pounds of apples
- Water bath canner
- Bowls
- 2 Canning jars, quart-sized
- 4 cups of water
- 1 cup of Sugar
- Citric acid (optional)
- Sharp knife

- Canning rings and seals
- Jar lifter
- Canning funnel
- Large spoons
- Towels
- Large pot

Method

1. First, you have to wash the apples and peel them. Take out the cores and slice the apples with the knife.

2. Citric acid can be used to prevent browning of the apples.

3. You have to make the syrup, which can be light or medium. Heat the water and add sugar into the saucepan. Wait for the sugar to dissolve.

4. Then pour this sugar syrup over the apples in the canning jars. Leave about half an inch of space in the can.

5. The canning rack should be placed on the water bath canner, above the water.

6. Air bubbles should be removed from the jars once they are full. There is a tool available for this.

7. Clean the rim of the canning jar to make sure there is no syrup. Then add the lid on top to seal it.

8. Once all the jars are packed with apples and syrup, you can lower them into the canner. Heat the water and process.

Preserved Tomatoes

Supplies

- 15 pounds of tomatoes
- 6 tbsp. canning salt
- 3/4 cup lemon juice
- Pressure canner
- 6 canning jars, quart-sized
- Sharp knife
- Canning lids
- Canning rings
- Bowls

- Towel
- Large pot
- Jar lifter
- Canning funnel
- Large spoon

Method

1. Blanch the tomatoes first. Depending on their size, you can do them a few at a time or all at once. Roma tomatoes are better for canning than most others, because they are smaller and meatier. You can do the blanching in a blancher or just with a pot of boiling water and spoon.

2. To can fresh tomatoes, they should be put in boiling water until the skin splits. This only takes a minute or less.

3. Then drop the tomatoes into a bowl of cold water immediately so that they stop cooking.

4. Take the skins off the tomatoes and cut them into quarters.

5. Then add the tomatoes into the jars.

6. Add lemon juice into the canning jars with 1 tsp of salt per quart of the jar.

7. Press down on the tomatoes so that there is lemon juice in the spaces between them. Only half an inch of headspace is required.

8. Once all the tomatoes are skinned, chopped and canned, get rid of any air bubbles.

9. Wipe the rims so that the food or juice doesn't affect the sealing process. Then add the lids on top and seal.

10. Place the jars in hot water in the canner. The water should not be boiling hot.

There are many other ways of canning or preserving foods that you can try.

Chapter Eleven: Seasonal Maintenance

Proper care and maintenance of the mini farm will ensure sustainability from season to season. Keeping coops and animal enclosures clean and properly prepared for winter months, depending on where you live, will prevent sickness and disease. Keeping on top of weeds and mulching plants will help to control disease.

Preparing Your Garden for Winter

Before winter sets in, the annual vegetables are near the end of their lifespan as they succumb to heavier frost. Spring and summer harvests have passed, and now you may want to let nature take its course in the garden for winter. However, your actions during this time will determine how much work you have to do once winter passes. If you just maintain your garden and take a few extra steps, you will have a lot less work in the long run.

Finished and Rotted Plants Should Be Cleaned Up

Leaving the finished or rotted plants in the garden will not only give an untidy appearance to your yard, but it will also harbor pests and diseases. Some insects lay eggs on plants during summer, and if you leave the plants there during winter, the insects will fester there until summer. Getting rid of these plants will help you to prevent pest infestations in spring. You can remove the plants or even bury them in the soil. Burying old plants will add organic matter and improve soil fertility.

Invasive Weeds Should be Removed

If some weeds invaded your garden in the growing season, now is the time to get rid of them. You can dig these up and burn them or throw them in the trash. A few varieties of weeds can also be used for compost. However, there are some that will grow in the compost heap as well. Don't throw the weeds away in some random area of the yard because they may just grow more there. Getting rid of them completely in winter is the best way to prevent their growth in the next crop season.

Prepare the Soil for Spring

Most people wait for spring to prepare the soil for the growing season. However, you can actually make use of the time during fall to do this. You can add manure, kelp, compost, bone meal, and rock phosphate to the soil. When you add these nutrients around the fall, it gives them enough time to break down and enrich the soil. They get biologically active and improve soil quality by the time spring comes around. If you work on the soil in spring, you waste time when you wait for the frost to dry out before you prepare the soil. If you amend and turn the soil in the fall, you will have finished half of the work before the busy season. Tilling your solid in fall will also improve drainage of the soil before extreme weather hits. After adding amendments to the soil, you can cover the yard with sheet plastic or any other covering that will prevent any winter rain from washing away the amendments. This covering is especially important for raised beds that drain easily. The rains can push the active ingredients below the root zone where the plants obtain nutrients. This sheeting can be removed in early spring. You can lightly till the soil at the time and prepare it for spring planting.

Plant Cover Crops

Late summer and early fall are a good time for sowing cover crops in some climates. These will help to protect the soil from erosion and will break the compacted soil up. It will also help to increase organic nutrients in the soil. Try growing legumes such as field peas or clover in your yard. These will increase nitrogen levels, which other vegetables benefit from. It is usually better to plant these cover crops about a month before the first heavy frost hits your area. There are some crops that can withstand even harsher conditions. You can check or ask other growers for recommendations on suitable cover crops in your region.

Prune Perennials

It is a good idea to trim some of your perennials in the fall. However, this should only be done for certain perennial plants and not all of them. Plants like fennel will do well with fall pruning. But plants such as blueberries and raspberries should be pruned in spring. Fall pruning should be done for herbs such as thyme, rosemary, and sage and vegetables such as rhubarb and asparagus. You can also clean up blackberry plants in the fall. If you get rid of the spent canes, it controls the vigorous spread of the plant.

Divide and Plant Bulbs

Most spring bulbs would have flowered and died by fall. However, there are some bulbs that bloom later, like lilies. About a month after their blooming, you can dig the plants up and divide any that seem straggly or crowded. Spring bulbs will require you to carry out some guesswork for this, but others are more obvious. You should dig at least five inches away from the stalk of the plant as you loosen the soil carefully. Gently lift up the bulbs and separate the bulblets so you can transplant them in other parts of the yard. You can plant your spring bulbs such as tulips and daffodils in fall as well.

Harvest the Compost and Regenerate More

Once the summer heat has passed, the microbes tend to hibernate in winter. However, you should not be ignoring the compost heap at this time, as you will miss a good opportunity. The material that you composted in the summer will be ready to be used by now. You can use this rich compost to cover the garden beds and amend any deficient soil. It will fertilize the soil in your yard and give a jumpstart to the growing season in spring. When you clean out the finished compost, you also get the chance to start a new batch that can be insulated against the cold winter. Add a lot of autumn leaves to your compost heap to keep the microbes active for a longer period. You can also add sawdust or straw along with food waste and any other active matter.

Replenish Mulch

Similar to summer mulching, winter mulching is also beneficial for your garden. It will help to prevent excess water loss and it also protects the soil from erosion. Mulching will inhibit the growth of weeds in your garden too. In addition to this, winter mulching has other benefits. The freezing weather of winter has an adverse effect on the plants and the soil. The heaving and churning will damage the roots. When you add a layer of mulch, it regulates the temperature of the soil, moisture levels, and also eases the transition to winter. You should add a thick mulch layer around your root vegetables in fall and winter, as it will prolong the crop and protect against hard frosts. While the mulch breaks down, new organic matter is added into the soil as well.

Assess the Growing Season

Take this time to assess the vegetables and fruits you planted in the last season. Did they grow well and give you enough produce? Take this time to reconsider any plants that have underperformed. You can look for varieties that might do better in your area as well. If certain plants did well, you could add some more varieties of the plants so that the harvest is extended. Take notes to see what worked in the last season and what did not. Assessing all this in the fall or winter gives you a better idea of what you should do in the next season.

Clean Your Tools

When your garden is in full swing, it can be hard to maintain the upkeep of all the tools or machinery. Fall is the best time to work on this. You can clean all the tools and sharpen them, so they perform better in the next season. It is important to clean and oil your tools from time to time so that they last longer. Get rid of any debris or dirt that might be stuck on your tools. A wire brush or sandpaper can be used for removing rust. A mill file will help you to sharpen the shovels and hoes. Once you do all this, use an oiled rag to rub over the surfaces. The machine oil will seal the metal and protect it from oxygen, which allows your tools to last much longer.

Regardless of what type of farm you have or where you live, it is better to do some seasonal maintenance. It will help your yard to do much better when spring and summer come around. It will also improve your soil and yield quality over time.

Chapter Twelve: Tracking Progress and Forming Community

Remember the importance of keeping plenty of notes to record your successes and failures to help ensure success for future endeavors. There is a vast array of resources available online, at the county agricultural extension, and through local farms. Other people who have mini farms are always willing to share what they've learned. By sharing information, you begin to see the importance of forming a community where you support each other in the good times and times of crisis.

A lot of information is available in books and on the Internet to help you get started with your mini farm. However, this information can often be generic and is usually aimed at a large audience. Building connections with other growers or farmers will be much more beneficial for you in the long run. Remember to track the progress of your farm as you work on it. You can share this information with other farmers when you connect.

While others may benefit from your learning experiences, you will also benefit from theirs. You will get to learn the same lingo that they use, when you form a community with them. While you will learn a lot as you work in the garden, it will save you a lot of time if you get advice from those with more experience. If you become a part of their community, they will be more than willing to help you avoid certain mistakes that they might have made in the past. They will also be happy to share some secrets of the trade that outsiders are not privy to.

If you don't connect with others, you will always remain on the outside. Forming a community will allow you to meet like-minded people and have a trustworthy group. You can rely on them for help and advice in your farming journey. They will also give you constructive feedback on what you do, so it helps you to grow and improve.

In this age of technology, you can benefit from the apps in this genre as well. There are some gardening apps that most efficient growers use these days:

Gardroid

It is a user-friendly app that has a large list of vegetables and fruits for you to look through. You can select some and add them to your garden list on the app. You can even track the progress of those crops on your app after you plant them in the garden. It has a calendar and notes section too.

Gardening Manager

This app will allow you to keep notes, track planting, or growing schedules, and keep other records. You can even take pictures from your garden and maintain a journal.

Plant Alarm

This app is used by gardeners to set alarms for their gardening activities. This allows you to ensure the proper care and maintenance of your plants. Don't rely on your memory to water your plants. Instead, you can set the alarm for each type of plant in the app. It will tell you exactly when and which plant you have to water on a daily basis.

Plant Diary

This simple app is great for tracking your garden's growth. There is a grid option that allows you to map out your actual garden in the app. You can record what you planted in a specific area of your yard. It is great for greenhouses, gardens, or farms. But this app is more beneficial for those who want a small garden in urban areas.

Garden Squared

This app helps you to plan your garden and track where and what you have planted. It also has a journal feature, which you can use to keep notes on the progress of any plants. This app does not have a database and is simpler than most other apps mentioned here.

Try downloading these apps on your phone or tablet to utilize their benefits. You can also join online forums or local farmers' associations to connect with others who enjoy gardening or farming.

Conclusion

Gardening is a great way to stay active and do something productive at the same time. With the help of *Mini Farming for Beginners: The Ultimate Guide to Remaking Your Backyard into a Mini Farm and Creating a Self-Sustaining Organic Garden*, you can now turn your backyard into a mini farm and enjoy the fruits of your labor throughout the year. It is a fulfilling activity that will keep you busy and also help you to ensure that you and your family eat healthy produce.

Producing your own food at home will contribute to financial and physical health. It has also been seen that people who practice gardening or farming are more in tune with nature, and this improves their mental wellbeing significantly.

Learning to grow your own food will reduce your dependency on commercial suppliers and save a lot of money. You can be reassured about the food you consume, since it will all be grown organically with your own hands. Corporate producers use various chemicals and pesticides that harm the environment and your health in the long run. This is why people have become more conscious of the importance of consuming organic food, and it is probably one reason why you want to grow your own garden. Working with the space you already have in your yard will allow you to utilize it in a way that benefits you on various fronts.

Even if you are a beginner at gardening and raising livestock, you can learn to do it successfully with the help of this book. As long as you put in a little work and invest your time in it, you will see your efforts pay off.

Good luck!

References

https://www.gardeningknowhow.com/special/organic/five-benefits-of-growing-an-organic-garden.htm

http://www.vegetable-gardening-with-lorraine.com/benefits-of-organic-gardening.html

https://www.motherearthnews.com/organic-gardening/gardening-techniques/crop-guide-growing-organic-vegetables-fruits-zl0z1211zsto

https://www.bhg.com/gardening/vegetable/vegetables/tips-for-growing-an-organic-vegetable-garden/

https://www.almanac.com/news/home-health/chickens/raising-chickens-101-how-get-started

https://morningchores.com/about-raising-pigs/

https://www.fromscratchmag.com/raise-cattle-small-acreage/

https://www.motherearthnews.com/homesteading-and-livestock/how-to-raise-honeybees-zmaz85zsie

https://homesteadsurvivalsite.com/common-garden-pests-deal-naturally/

https://dengarden.com/pest-control/Natural-Garden-Pest-Control

https://www.goodhousekeeping.com/home/gardening/a20705991/garden-insect-pests/

https://kidsgardening.org/gardening-basics-dealing-with-garden-pests-and-diseases/

https://www.gardeningchannel.com/organic-pest-and-disease-control/

https://www.thespruce.com/groundhog-damage-in-yard-2131141

http://npic.orst.edu/pest/wildyard.html

https://www.motherearthnews.com/organic-gardening/growing-season-zmaz94jjzraw

https://www.theprairiehomestead.com/2019/09/extend-garden-season.html

https://www.gardeners.com/how-to/season-extending-techniques/5063.html

https://www.youtube.com/watch?v=VpVOoTF8124

https://hudsonvalleykitchens.com/2017/09/22/preparing-for-the-season-of-harvest/

https://www.youtube.com/watch?v=9y5vivDjAm4

https://www.amodernhomestead.com/how-to-prepare-for-the-harvest/

https://melissaknorris.com/how-to-organize-build-your-homestead-food-storage-kitchen/

https://15acrehomestead.com/harvest-season/

https://www.wikihow.com/Build-a-Shed

https://morningchores.com/chicken-coop-plans/

https://modernfarmer.com/2015/09/how-to-build-a-chicken-coop/

https://www.popularmechanics.com/home/a26063857/diy-greenhouse/

https://greenhouseplanter.com/how-to-build-a-hoop-house/

https://www.goodhousekeeping.com/home/gardening/a20706669/how-to-build-compost-bin/

https://www.youtube.com/watch?v=Pi1x-kyC49o

https://backyardfarming.blogspot.com/2016/04/off-site-gardening-factors-to-consider.html

https://www.pinterest.com/pin/63261569752809153/

https://articles.bplans.com/how-to-start-a-farm-and-how-to-start-farming/

https://www.thespruce.com/how-to-start-a-small-farm-3016691

https://www.countryfarm-lifestyles.com/Mini-Farms.html

https://www.motherearthliving.com/gardening/backyard-farm-zmfz15mfzhou

https://homesteadlaunch.com/backyard-farming/

https://www.ecohome.net/guides/2228/grow-food-at-home-7-tips-for-growing-food-in-small-spaces/

https://commonsensehome.com/home-food-preservation/

https://www.motherearthnews.com/real-food/how-to-preserve-food-zm0z71zsie

https://originalhomesteading.com/ways-to-preserve-food/

https://preparednessmama.com/canning-equipment/

https://www.britannica.com/topic/smoking-food-preservation

https://www.simplycanning.com/home-canning-recipes.html

https://www.goodhousekeeping.com/cooking-tools/g30200878/best-food-dehydrator/

https://www.urbangardensweb.com/2013/02/03/10-tips-for-maintaining-a-healthy-garden/

https://www.thespruce.com/vegetable-garden-maintenance-1403170

https://www.finegardening.com/article/10-ways-to-keep-your-garden-healthy

https://learn.eartheasy.com/articles/ten-ways-to-prepare-your-garden-for-winter/

https://www.almanac.com/content/preparing-your-garden-winter

https://learn.compactappliance.com/apps-for-gardeners/

https://commonsensehome.com/gardening-journal-templates/

https://www.backyardgardener.com/garden-interest/plant-finder/5-benefits-of-connecting-with-other-gardeners-through-a-small-online-community/

https://www.treehugger.com/lawn-garden/10-online-gardening-communities-you-should-join.html

Here's another book by Dion Rosser
that you might be interested in

Printed in Great Britain
by Amazon

35734534R00063